Praise for *Muster D*

'Kick your boots off and settle in for a wild journey of love and heartbreak, from the most inspiring cattlewoman I know' – Margareta Osborne, author and grazier

'This book is an evocative, authentic, and freshly engaging account of pastoral life from a young woman brought up on a cattle station in far outback Western Australia. Honest and matter-of-fact as befits such an upbringing, it reads at times like a Wild West adventure story as the girl grows into a woman managing a half-million acre station. As a result, *Muster Dogs* also provides a unique insight into the wonderful world of working dogs, their personalities and attributes, and farming life in remote, sometimes dangerous country' – Charles Massy, author and voice for regenerative agriculture

Aticia Grey grew up from the age of five on the family's cattle station in the far southwest Pilbara. After attending boarding school for the required years, she returned home to work on the land alongside her parents and brother. Twenty-seven years later, she is still there with her partner, Adam, and her mother, Susan, managing the property with a tireless team of kelpies and practising her rain dance. Whenever she gets a chance outside station work, she can be found taking photos of her dogs, organising new homes nationally and internationally for her pups, reading anything in fiction she can get her hands on, and cooking up something unhealthy in the kitchen.

pilbaraworkingdogs.com
facebook.com/pilbaraworkingdogs
instagram.com/pilbaraworkingdogs

Aticia Grey

MUSTER DOGS

An outback story of red dirt, kelpies
and the future of a family farm

ABC
BOOKS

The ABC 'Wave' device is a trademark of the
Australian Broadcasting Corporation and is used
under licence by HarperCollins*Publishers* Australia.

HarperCollins*Publishers*
Australia • Brazil • Canada • France • Germany • Holland • Hungary
India • Italy • Japan • Mexico • New Zealand • Poland • Spain • Sweden
Switzerland • United Kingdom • United States of America

First published in Australia in 2021
by HarperCollins*Publishers* Australia Pty Limited
Level 13, 201 Elizabeth Street, Sydney NSW 2000
ABN 36 009 913 517
harpercollins.com.au

A catalogue record for this book is available from the National Library of Australia.

ISBN 978 0 7333 4158 8 (paperback)
ISBN 978 1 4607 1353 2 (ebook)

Cover design by Andy Warren, HarperCollins Design Studio
Front cover image by Steve Strike / Ambience Entertainment
Back cover image by Aticia Grey
Photo on page iii of Aticia Grey and her dogs in South Australia after their goat-mustering
adventures by Lachlan Douglas
All uncredited photos by Aticia Grey

Typeset in Sabon LT by Kirby Jones
Printed and bound in Australia by McPherson's Printing Group

*To the amazing workings dogs who help shape
Australia. Giving their all and asking nothing in
return except a feed, a pat and the chance to do it
all again tomorrow.*

*May they get the recognition, appreciation
and respect they deserve.*

Contents

Prologue 1

1. Barefoot Bush Kid 5

2. For the Love of Dogs 26

3. Early Days 35

4. The Next Generation 50

5. The Dog World 65

6. Student First, Teacher Second 72

7. Pilbara Working Dogs 93

8. Kelpies and Country Girls 101

9. Life Lessons and Learning Curves 121

10. Miles and Memories 141

11. Pups and Pedigrees 152

12. The Start of the Storm 164

13. Predators and Predation 181

14. The Devastation of Drought 194

15. The Heat of Winter 203

16. Gossip Girl 224

17. Muster Dogs 242

18. The Other Side 260

Teesh's Tips and Tricks 271

Acknowledgements 289

Prologue

If someone had said to me seven years ago that I would soon own twelve kelpies and six maremmas, be managing our family cattle station and writing a book, I would have thought they'd lost their mind. Now, most days I wonder if I've lost mine.

Though it's had its up and downs, I wouldn't trade my life for anything. My dogs have taught me to be a better person, to be more accepting of situations I can't control and that there really is more to life than the station I grew up on. They gave me the confidence to travel to different parts of Australia on two truly 'once in a lifetime' road trips. They inspired my travels overseas to America and Alaska where I was able to see working dogs in completely different situations, invaluable and incredible in their own right. They connected me to a whole new world of like-minded folk who share the same passion and appreciation for these amazing animals as I do. They have helped me find my independence, running my own business alongside my family's. But most of all, in my dogs, I have found my passion. No matter where we are in life, as long as I have my dogs by my side, I am home. And that is the greatest gift of all.

Through this book, I tell my story of life in the rugged Pilbara region of Western Australia, learning to run a half-a-million-acre cattle station through some of the hardest years my family has experienced, and how my working dogs proved essential players in that time and continue to do so as we transition into the future. It's a story of how my dogs filled a void in my life before I even realised there was something missing; it's about the mistakes I've made along the way, the lessons I've learnt and how the experiences I've had have shaped the direction of the path I am on today. It's a path that will have many twists, turns and, no doubt, bumps too, but one that excites me when I think about the possibilities for the future.

One of the dogs you will meet on this journey is Gossip Girl, the beautiful pup featured with her siblings in the ABC's *Muster Dogs* documentary about our first nine months together.

This isn't a manual on how to train a dog. Far from it. But through my experiences, I'll share different techniques that have worked for me. And some that haven't. There are many talented people I have met who have gained more knowledge, experience and understanding of dogs over the years than I will likely ever know. And I'm grateful for that. I appreciate the opportunity this offers me to continue to learn from those folk even as I tread my own unique path.

Life isn't a destination. It's the journey we are on right now and who could ask for better company on the ride than the unquestioning enthusiasm of a loyal dog.

Thank you for joining me.

Chapter One

Barefoot Bush Kid

'If the ground's hot, run from cow pat to cow pat.
Just try to avoid the wet ones.'
— Eight-year-old station girl who looked suspiciously like me

I was a typical bush kid growing up. Barefoot, covered in a permanent layer of red dust from head to toe, hair a scraggy mess. Prickles were a constant companion. I spent half my time pulling them out of my feet, the other half dragging my feet across the ground trying the cheat's way of dislodging them. Although I had earnt the nickname of Speedy Spider Legs, my brother was still faster than me and my fallback strategy to escape his pursuit was running off the lawn and up the rocky hill. Honestly, I'm sure life would have been easier if I'd just worn shoes, but my tough feet became a point of personal pride.

My hair was a completely different matter. It has always been long and as I grew older, I appreciated that feminine trait in a masculine world. But as a kid, it was nothing more than a nuisance. After its weekly wash, I would sit in front of Dad while he watched the evening news and his work-roughened hands would gently untangle the knots out of my dark locks. Mum would corner me next morning and firmly secure it in a plait. I'd jam my hat on and forget about it until there was more out of the plait than in it, and the process would start all over again.

I wasn't born into station life, not literally like my mum was. In too much of a hurry to wait for hospital, she was born on the side of the road under a tree on the way into Port Hedland from the station her parents were managing at the time. We moved up to the family cattle station in the southwest Pilbara of Western Australia from Perth when I was five, after purchasing Glen Florrie off my dad's parents. My brother, Murray, and I are fourth-generation pastoralists on my mother's side, but both our parents had grown up on stations at either end of Western Australia's pastoral country. When the opportunity arose to shift the trucking business they had built from the ground up and move back out to the bush, my parents grabbed it. They wanted Murray and me to grow up the same way they had, and did what they could to make it happen.

I was not impressed with the move to Glen Florrie. Averse to change, and with a healthy stubborn streak, when we arrived at our new home, I refused to get out of the bunk of the truck until it eventually got too warm inside and I had to concede defeat. But I very soon learnt to love the new life I was granted.

Our early childhood was spent split between the station and the truck, as my parents ran both businesses together. The four of us spent many a day covering a lot of miles in the truck, Mum and Dad taking turns behind the wheel. They bought a Scania prime mover the same year I was born and commissioned an artist to paint an image of outback Australia on both doors and a sketch that my uncle had drawn on the roof. This image of a galloping bull with a stockman on a horse riding close alongside has always been one of my favourites. I found the draft sketch a few years ago in amongst some old papers and had it framed and placed on the wall, old coffee stains and all.

The Scania, easily recognisable by the 'Drover's Dream' scripted across the top of the cab, was our second home. She had an extended bunk built inside so there was room for all of us to sleep, and I still marvel at how my parents managed it. As Murray and I got bigger, Dad would often opt to sleep in the driver's seat rather than try to wrangle space in the bunk.

In the early days, Dad built a sandpit under the bunk for my brother to play in during the long trips. It was later

The Scania in its prime.

converted to house a small TV and a video player, and many a mile was driven with us kids hanging our heads over the edge of the bunk or twisted around in the passenger seat so we could watch movies. I spent so much of my early childhood in that beautiful old truck that the noise of the engine became a normal part of my world. I would climb into the truck and not ten minutes into the trip would be asleep in the bunk, lulled by the motor and the familiar rhythm of the gear changes. Years later when I was battling homesickness at boarding school, I would listen to the road trains rolling past on the highway and imagine I was back out on the road with Dad again. Who knew the sound of a Jake Brake could be solace for a kid's soul?

My love of trucks never diminished and a few years ago, I finally realised my dream of getting my own multi-combination licence, which allows me to drive road trains with multiple trailers along the highway. Though most of my truck driving is spent carting cattle between paddocks on the station rather than on bitumen, it's still one of my proudest achievements.

*

Station life as a kid was wonderful. To many visitors who came by, I'm sure it seemed my main mission in life was to be underfoot as much as I could – usually with a menagerie of animals in tow. Murray and I had only each other for company much of the time, which, contrary to a lot of siblings it seems, kept the bond between us strong. Murray was always very sensible and mature for his age, as demonstrated when we spent six months living on a farm near Geraldton before our move to the station. Murray was just five years old when he would get three-year-old me up and breakfasted, collect the 'smoko' (morning tea) Mum had prepared earlier, then deliver it on his three-wheeler motorbike, with me on the back, to where Mum was out working at the cattle yards. This role of protector continued throughout our childhood while I played the cheeky ratbag befitting of the youngest child. In later years, I could be found running around with a swear jar to catch the ringers out with any bad language, and also playing tricks, usually involving water, on our unsuspecting visitors.

We didn't have 24-hour power for most of my childhood; we only had electricity when the generator ran, three hours in the morning and three hours at night – enough to keep the fridges and freezers cool. This meant no electricity during the hottest part of the day nor at night when the summer heat would linger endlessly. One memorable new year was welcomed in with a lovely 49 degrees on the verandah at 1 am, while the daytime highs were nudging low 50s in the shade. Not pleasant.

At night Mum, Murray and I would put our beds out on the lawn, in the hope of catching a breeze, while Dad sweated

Murray and me, heading to the yards with smoko.

it out on the verandah. Wet towels would provide some relief or, if we were really desperate, we'd place our beds under the sprinkler. We were joined on the lawn by calves, pet joeys and dogs. I recall on more than one occasion waking up to a calf casually chewing on my hair. I wasn't kidding about the state of it. When the mosquitoes were bad, we'd burn green coils in an attempt to deter them. Even now the smell of mosquito coils takes me back to those nights spent out under the stars.

With no power during the day, Murray and I couldn't spend hours on the old Nintendo or in front of the TV watching cartoons, so we had to find other ways to entertain ourselves. We have a large number of date palms in the river behind our homestead and often we would go exploring down where the hanging fronds made cool caves. We had our motorbikes – a two-wheel PeeWee 80 and a three-wheeler with a plastic seat mounted on the back for a passenger, usually me. When the heat outside was unbearable, we would sit on the cool (it's all relative) cement floor in the old brick section of the homestead and pass many an hour playing cards and board games.

My brother's love of Lego, which kept him so entertained during his early years, has continued through to his adult life, as has my love of reading books. Even now, when I get caught up in a good book and the clock slowly ticks late into the night, I can hear my mum's voice echoing from my childhood, 'Put the book down, you won't get up in the morning.'

I often claim we only have two seasons in the Pilbara, a hot summer and a warm winter. The latter is beautifully mild and lasts about four months, just long enough to remind us why we like living here before the long summer grind begins again. We have always tried to do the majority of our cattle work during the cooler months. Though there are benefits to waiting for it to warm up – like fewer helicopter hours due to the cattle being contained close to water and cleaner musters with not as many missed – it can be hard on stock and stockmen/women alike. So we try to have most of our cattle work wrapped up before the worst of the heat arrives and the crew heads off. With the exception of an occasional full-time employee, most of our crew were and still are seasonal, helping us with fencing, repairs and maintenance of watering points and, of course, cattle mustering.

Winter would find us with a full crew around, and friends and family passing through, especially in the holidays. The supposed isolation of the property felt like a myth! By the end of a busy season, peppered with social events like gymkhanas and rodeos, summer was almost a welcome relief, as it offered us a chance to have just our family at home for a while, waiting for the cyclones to roll in and deliver some beautiful rain.

Though our best chance of a wet season is generally summer, the location of our property means we can either get summer rain, winter rain, both or, as we experienced again in recent years, neither. As with most areas of Australia, rain

Mum and Jenny, our neighbour, crossing the running river.

is never guaranteed but, in general, summer rains deliver the feed and winter rains deliver the wildflowers. Cyclones are prayed for by property owners; the bountiful feed they might provide from a decent fall of rain worth the risk of damage they can inflict. As kids, we were taught to love and respect the power of the weather.

Growing up, the rule for floodwaters was 'If you can't walk across it, don't drive across it' and we still live by that today. During the wet season, we can be cut off from the highway for weeks at a time. In the earlier years, it was hard to keep veggies fresh with limited power, so a well-stocked storeroom full of tinned and dry food was essential. In the event food stores ran low and our rivers were running high, we would meet the neighbours at the banks and ferry stores across the swirling water by stringing a rope over the river and hoisting boxes up onto the shoulders of the menfolk who waded back and forth. Or, if our station grader was close at hand and the current not too strong for it, we would fire it up to carry the food supplies across with a little less legwork.

It isn't just during the summer wet season that our rivers can run. As freshly licensed teenagers, we got a winter downpour while at the local gymkhana and had a slippery drive in our holden utes back to the neighbours' place. There we met Dad and a family friend, Gary, who had come out in four-wheel-drives to pick us up, leaving a grader waiting at the river. It was lucky they did, because the Wannery Creek, which runs behind our homestead, was on the rise. By the time we got to the creek, we had to chain the utes to the back of the grader and tow them across the rising water one at a time. It was a spooky feeling floating along behind the grader, feeling the ute being swept downstream in the current and the chain pulling taut. We made it, just, with the last vehicle getting towed to the homestead side of the river just as the water reached the grader's limits. Finally, after a long day navigating a route that would normally take three hours, we could relax and enjoy the rain from the comfort of our verandah.

*

Checking the rain gauge was one of our favourite jobs as kids. We would race up the hill to be the first to pull the tin lid off the canister, rudely dislodging any resident geckos and frogs. In the big rains, we'd ride our bikes down to the river crossing nearby to check the flood levels and monitor if the water was rising over or receding from our last carefully placed rock marker. Rains were, and always will be, big cause for celebration. We never know when the next downpour might come or how long the current one might last. The low roar of a strong-flowing river is a powerful reminder of Mother Nature's dangerous unpredictability. In drought-prone country, we soon learnt to appreciate every drop you get, no matter how ill-timed it might be. There is no better reason than life-giving rain to change your plans, and no better feeling than watching the country respond to a drink with a flourish.

With the instalment of solar power in 2000, the same year I headed off to boarding school, we were finally able to at least run fans overnight (if the batteries held out) and our fridges could run full-time. This seemed like true luxury after growing up with no power at all for most of the day. It was 20 years later, only a few months before Christmas of 2020, that we finally upgraded our solar system to be large enough to accommodate air-conditioning. Now that we have it, I really don't know how we survived so many years without it.

*

Murray and I were home-schooled through Carnarvon School of the Air, one of the last generations of students taught via radio before it was replaced by the internet. We would have half-hour air lessons each morning with the teacher and others in our class then spend the rest of the school day filling in our workbooks. Mum was our teacher for most of the year, but we occasionally had governesses or volunteer REVISE teachers to help her out. I probably owe most of them an apology. Where Murray was the perfect student, I was most definitely not. If there was cattle work going on outside, or even if there wasn't, I wanted to be out there. I spent most of my energy trying to make that happen, or with my nose buried in a book, usually one of Mum's forbidden Mills & Boons. My love of reading was most definitely inherited. The best part about our schooling was being able to complete work ahead of time so we could be out taking our place with the mustering team. School would often follow us out to stock camp, but it could usually be wrapped up in a few hours and an air lesson could be taken via a radio hooked up to the ute's battery.

For my tenth birthday, I was thoroughly spoilt when I received my chestnut gelding, Bucky Boy, and a little yellow Datsun car. The Datsun had actually been purchased for its motor, which would eventually end up in a bull wagon I could take out mustering, but the car turned up around my birthday so I claimed it. Until the motor transplant occurred, I had my own wheels and I was chuffed – peeling paint, rusted floor and all. I used to do laps up and down the airstrip, teaching visiting friends and cousins how to drive. Its 'garage' was the old blacksmith's shop that doubled as Mum's gardening shed. There was just enough room to squeeze the car in alongside the old anvil mounted on a wooden stump and the shovels and pots housed on the other side. I used to take great pride in carefully reversing in, even though it would have been much easier to drive forward, but my reversing skills benefited from the practice. I even took the cops for a drive in my pride and joy. The Pannawonica police used to visit nearby stations each year and it was always a cause of great excitement for us kids. In exchange for my chauffeuring, they would take Murray and

Mustering interrupted by School of the Air lessons.

me for a drive in their police wagon with sirens blaring and lights flashing. They would overnight with us, playing cricket in the afternoon and card games at night. One visit, I caught them cheating during a game and claimed they were 'shonky cops!', much to the amusement of everyone present.

*

The difference between Murray's and my personalities was probably most obvious when it came to socialising. Murray craved the company of other kids and would drive himself 70 kilometres along our gravel driveway in his bull wagon to the neighbours' place for a game of cricket. In contrast, I was happy at home with my four-legged friends. I always had an assortment of calves, dogs, joeys, pet chooks, guinea pigs and horses around me. After Murray headed to boarding school when he was twelve years old, I relied on my animals even more for company. During the holidays when he came home I would get trained up in either Aussie rules football or cricket depending on the season, and by the time I felt like I was getting the hang of one, it was shelved for the other. I learnt early on that Murray is a brilliant teacher and, though I was a terrible student, his patience with my lack of patience was admirable. It still is.

When it was my turn to go to boarding school in Perth in Year 8, I didn't adapt well to the change. All of a sudden, I had no animals nearby, no freedom and, worst of all, I had to wear shoes … everywhere! The dull ache of homesickness was constant. I didn't fit in with other kids my age; I was a quiet country girl who wasn't up with fashion or sports. My tape player in all its multi-coloured glory on the desk near my bed drew a bit of teasing. But I had 'won' that for 'best horse stack' at our local gymkhana after falling off Bucky Boy. It held a place of pride as evidence of my injury: a broken collarbone. The old-fashioned country music that came out of my player didn't help my cause for fitting in much either.

As big of an adjustment as my new living arrangements were, school itself was a shock to the system. I had gone from School of the Air – with the total number of students barely reaching 50, seven in my year, and only me in my classroom once Murray left – to Governor Stirling Senior High School with 1200 students and classes of 30. The kids loved to speculate on the rumour that 'Govo' was originally designed as a prison and I could believe it with its imposing brick walls and stark design.

Every night I would be on the phone to my parents, desolate at the isolation I ironically had never felt at home. I can appreciate now how hard it must have been for them to listen to my miserable recounts of the day's activities and despair at what I was missing out on at home. Mum had experienced boarding school herself when she was my age, though in those days, they could only head home for the long summer holidays and correspondence was limited to letters in the mail. Dad had left school at the end of Year 7, after falling nearly four months behind in his study while working on his home station, Thangoo. At that time, there was no option to continue high school by correspondence; it would have required moving into Broome and he was needed at the station. I did have another option, though: completing high school via School of Isolated Distance Education, which would have allowed me to remain at Glen Florrie. Dad was fine with this, as was I, but Mum rightly maintained that I needed to experience boarding school. Eventually, after yet another teary phone call with my parents, Dad offered me a deal. I just had to finish the first half of the year at boarding school and if I still hated it, I could come home. Bingo, I finally had an end date! I knew that I would be home at the end of second term, there was no way I would want to stay, so I just had to make it through until then.

Suddenly, school didn't seem so bad; it was only temporary, after all. The other girls in my dorm were lovely and I was starting to learn to mix with kids my own age, a skill I had not yet mastered. My calls to home became less tearful and I slowly started to find my place in my new world. I took up netball and tried my hand at cricket. There were moments when it was almost enjoyable, but nothing could eclipse my love of station life.

Finally, the promised deadline arrived but just as escape seemed within my grasp, Dad dispelled it with a few quiet words. 'Sorry, kid, you like it there now, so you have to stay.' I couldn't argue, I didn't hate it anymore, though I would never grow to love it like Murray did. Well played, Dad, well played.

As hard as the early years of boarding school were, school itself was relatively easy, as our home-schooling had put us a year ahead of the current curriculum. I made friends with some of the 'Day Bugs' in my year, as the kids who didn't board were known to those of us who did, while our nickname was 'Swanleigh Scabs'. It was fairly earnt; we were masters at begging for food or spare money to buy from the school's canteen. We were fed well, but at the time, we didn't think so. The sandwiches we could order from the boarding house each evening at dinner were doled out in the morning at breakfast, unappetisingly bland. The best strategy was to order ham and cheese, leave it in the fridge at the boarding house and hope that you could 'scab' something for lunch at school to tide you over till you could cook up toasties when you got home.

My favourite class of all was Home Economics where we got to cook something once a fortnight. Our pocket money for the week never seemed enough to buy more than the absolutely necessary two-minute noodles we lived on, chewing gum and chocolate. All the important stuff. Noodles especially were valuable currency for bartering – the loan of a shirt for the night or a bite of someone else's chocolate stash.

Where I struggled, Murray thrived. He made friends easily and his love of sports only grew. Part way through my three years boarding at Swanleigh, I started visiting family friends who had a small property nearby with a paddock full of exceptionally good polocrosse horses. I would spend every weekend I could and two afternoons a week having riding lessons and learning to swing a racquet. I was given one of their beautiful horses as a birthday present and started competing in a few polocrosse games. But I've never been competitive and my favourite times were the casual training days in the paddock, throwing a ball around, working on my riding skills and enjoying the wonderful company. The beautiful property became my second home and our friendship continued long past my boarding-school years.

Even though boarding school had become tolerable, I never really enjoyed living in the city, so I headed to Narrogin Agriculture College south of Perth to complete my Years 11 and 12 schooling. It wasn't as good as home but at least it was back in the country. I was one of the first girls to attend the college without signing up for the equine course, preferring to learn other skills like preg-testing and artificial insemination in cattle. I had my first experience in a shearing shed and I absolutely loved the atmosphere, the unique lanolin smell and the novelty of working with animals that couldn't hurt me. My shearing skills weren't going to take me far, though, with my best efforts capping out at about twenty head of sheep shorn in a day.

When I got my P plates and a second-hand VS Holden Commodore ute in Year 12, I could drive myself to and from the station each school holidays. The freedom was amazing.

As hard as boarding school was, especially that first year which I can honestly say I wouldn't want to go through again, I am glad that I experienced it. Station life had taught us resilience, responsibility and common sense but I was missing other life skills I needed to know. I had never learnt to interact with kids my own age, preferring the company of adults or younger kids when I'd had to attend annual school camps. Living away from home taught me how to cope with a city lifestyle and showed me that there was a world outside of the station. As good as it was to experience, though, I couldn't wait to get home.

Chapter Two

For the Love of Dogs

**'Love completely while you can, so you don't carry
the burden of regret when you can't.'**
– Hindsight

I don't ever recall a time in my life when we didn't have dogs as part of our family, along with an assortment of other animals. When we lived in Perth, Murray and I had guinea pigs that we loved alongside a beautiful old German shepherd called Sheba and a spritely little cream corgi, Cherry. I always enjoyed hearing the story of the meter man having a run-in with them at our suburban home. After reading the neighbours' meter, Meter Man jumped the fence into our yard, tripped over the corgi and got bailed up by the German shepherd. When he dusted himself off, unharmed but with a dented ego, and complained that the dogs needed to be tied up, Dad remarked that he should have used the gate like any non-intruder would do. I still laugh at the image of the dogs working as a very mismatched team to protect their yard from the meter man.

Both dogs moved to the station with us but Sheba's hips started giving her trouble not long after we arrived. One day in summer, Sheba and Cherry followed us out for a ride on our horses through the paddocks, as they often did. Old Sheba was starting to slow as arthritis took hold and we lost track of them as we rode further out. We got home late in the afternoon with no sign of the dogs, despite our best attempts to find them. A summer storm came up later that evening and had all the creeks flowing quickly. Though Cherry made it home overnight, Old Sheba was never found. We don't know to this day if she was swept away in the rushing water trying to cross a swollen creek or if a heart attack claimed her in the end. I still have a strong love of beautiful German shepherds, loyal and protective to the core.

*

When I was seven, I was finally able to reach the foot pedals in one of the bull wagons (if I perched right on the edge of the seat and stretched out my toes), so it was time to learn to drive. This was a big step up from just being able to steer vehicles from Dad's lap and I was equal parts excited and nervous, as I took my place in the wagon, ready to drive it the few kilometres home. But using the clutch proved too much and I kept stalling each time I tried to start. So Dad got the buggy trundling down the road in first gear, and I slid across into the driver's seat as Dad jumped out. I was driving! Until I reached a gate where I stalled the buggy each time and Dad, following along steadily behind in the grader, would get me going again (in second gear now because I complained that first was way too slow) and the pattern would repeat. By the time I made it home, there was a fair bit of heat coming out from under the bonnet of the poor vehicle, which hadn't appreciated my high revs, but I didn't mind the ribbing I received because finally I could drive!

The little dog riding shotgun with me through this momentous occasion was my little chihuahua cross girl called Gem. We had selected Gem as a pup on a trip to Perth and she was the perfect little mate. Though she didn't look much like a robust station dog with her cream coat, fine legs and large, perpetually weeping eyes, she was a tough little thing. She and another dog followed a geologist in his car 32 kilometres one day before we finally caught up with the two tired and thirsty wanderers. We eventually drilled a bore in the area where we found them and it is still called Gem's Mill in her honour.

Gem was a great mate, loyally keeping me company on any number of adventures. Unfortunately, I lost her too early and it was one of the hardest losses of my childhood. On the fateful day, I was charged with finding the horses, so I headed out on the motorbike just before lunch. Gem tried to follow me but I called over my shoulder for her to stay home. I wanted to ride faster than she could safely handle so that I could be back quicker. I remember looking back and seeing her standing halfway along the track, watching me ride off.

While out looking for the horses, I noticed two wedge-tailed eagles flying in the area and alarm bells went off. These birds aren't prolific on our property, but I knew that my small cream dog would be the perfect prey for them if she was out there.

I flew back into the house in a panic, frantically asking Mum where Gem was. Her reply confirmed my fears. 'I haven't seen her, Teesh.'

With dawning horror, I tore back out on the bike, desperately hoping I would find my dog safe and sound. What felt like a lifetime later, I spotted her dog shape but I was too late. She had fallen victim to the large predators, who reluctantly left their meal as I rode over, tears already streaming down my face. My gorgeous little dog's loyalty had cost her her life.

Gem's death stayed with me for a long time. A lot of my guilt lay in not taking her that day like she was asking or, at the very least, making sure she couldn't follow. But guilt also lay in knowing I hadn't given her enough attention. Another very cute pup I had adopted from a litter Mum had bred had taken much of the time and attention that should have been Gem's. I knew deep down that it hadn't been fair on my older dog. It was a hard lesson to learn but an important one.

It wasn't just dogs I grew strongly attached to. Both our parents taught Murray and me early on the importance of compassion. I loved caring for orphan kangaroos with Mum and we often had one or more joeys hanging in a makeshift pouch off the back of a chair around the house. They would start heading bush as they got older, coming back less and less until finally we lost touch with most, but it was still a rewarding experience. Raising poddy calves was my real passion, though, one I shared with Mum. Dad would often bring home a sick calf that needed hand-rearing, and when they were really struggling, Mum would get up at all hours of the night to tend to them. Once I was old enough, I would help share the late-night load. Some calves were found severely dehydrated, malnourished and in bad shape. We learnt to rehydrate slowly, tackle infections early and that sometimes the kindest gift you can give is the mercy of a quick goodbye. Some of these orphaned calves were the result of dingo attacks. The injuries inflicted by dingoes can be brutal and often lead to terrible infections deep in the muscle that require regular cleaning and antibiotics. I grew up with a strong resentment of dingoes after losing many a pet calf to them over the years. It has only been since I have had my working dogs and learnt a few life

Easton and Corbin enjoying Mum's affection.

lessons from them about perspective that my resentment has changed to respect.

*

My first kelpie, Joy, was a straight red colour with a splash of white on her chest. She was an energetic and highly affectionate girl who followed me everywhere I went, sometimes to our detriment. One afternoon, I was tearing around in a fit of excitement waiting for our School of the Air teachers to arrive for their annual visit. There is a hill where our water tank sits that affords you a look along the driveway to spot early signs of an arriving vehicle. I had already worn a pad between the house and the top of the hill with my little PeeWee 80 motorbike, checking for their dust. Joy and I headed back up for another look because surely they weren't far away by now. It was near the generator shed that Joy ran across in front of me and I collected her with my front tyre, sending us both flying. Luckily Joy escaped with no noticeable injuries while I limped my way back to the house with blood pouring down my knees. Of course, it was while I was being patched up by my ever patient mother that the teachers finally arrived. As a kid I was always so proud of my battle scars and to this day, my knees still sport the evidence of that misadventure.

*

I had a not so pleasant experience with a kelpie when I was much younger. I have only some hazy memory of the incident, but Mum recalls it in much more detail.

'You were three. We had gone to the station to pick up cattle with the truck and were visiting your aunt and uncle, who were managing Glen Florrie for your grandad. The dog was a big red-and-tan male kelpie, Syd. You were just a littlie, out there playing with your older cousin. We heard you screaming and I went running out. There was blood, but I couldn't see where it was coming from. I grabbed you and put you up on the kitchen bench so we could see the injury and clean it. We were just so grateful it missed your carotid artery, Teesh. If it had got that artery, you wouldn't have had a hope.'

My memory is of being dragged around the lawn by my hair. I still have the scars where his teeth punctured the skin under my ear. Why that dog attacked me, I'll never know. Maybe he thought I was a threat to his mistress, maybe he was joining in on the game. Either way, it was a lucky escape but it didn't stop me from developing an amazing love for this beautiful breed of dog as my life continued.

*

Those early animals taught me so much about being responsible for another living creature and the importance of empathy. Though it was hard losing animals we had invested so much time and affection in, I wouldn't have wanted my childhood to have been without them. I remember reaching a crossroads after the loss of a beloved pet, for once from old age, when I was a teenager. I realised I could protect myself from the pain of losing a companion by holding back my feelings, making it easier on me when the time came. Or I could love them for all it was worth while I had them and, though the pain would be sharper, I would enjoy the memories without regret when they passed on. I chose the latter and have never regretted that decision.

Chapter Three

Early Days

'In a good season, this country can fatten a broomstick.'
– Murray Grey

Our property, Glen Florrie Station, also known as Glenflorrie, is located in the southwest Pilbara of Western Australia. It's a beautiful station surrounded by picturesque ranges featuring stunning gorges with creeks and rivers winding through. It's not an easy station by any means, earning itself a reputation over the years as a battler's block. It has very little soft river-flood country but its harshness has its own beauty. From spinifex-covered hills and mulga flats to creeks lined with majestic river gums, paperbarks and abundant bird life, it's the type of country that captures a piece of your heart in the good times and can bring you to your knees in the bad.

Glen Florrie was originally purchased by Grandad Grey as a fattening block for sale cattle, with its position south of the tick line and closer to Perth affording easier access to markets. The cattle he sent down from the family's home property, Thangoo Station, located just south of Broome, did well on the different types of shrubs and grasses that were on offer at Glen Florrie. When Grandad owned Glen Florrie, he preferred to gather the cattle in to select those ready for sale by trapping, rather than mustering. Trapping is still used as an effective mustering method on Thangoo today. He had wire yards built on many of the water points with 'spear traps' strategically placed which allowed the cattle to enter the yards for a drink, but not leave again. It's a very cost-effective way to gather cattle as long as there is no other ground water outside the traps they can drink from, like puddles from an unexpected storm. Glen Florrie also has a number of permanent pools and fresh-water springs throughout the river and creek systems, which means some areas can't be trapped easily.

Once the cattle were trapped into the wire yards, they were sorted into two mobs through a single-file 'race', with sale cattle being trucked to the homestead while the others were 'bushed' back out into the paddock. Though economical, this brisk handling method didn't encourage quiet or cooperative cattle and they disappeared back out into the scrub at pace.

What also didn't help the temperament of the cattle was the cull, or sale, cows Dad's older brother sent down from his herd on the part of Thangoo he had taken on. He had a coding system where code 1s were his good breeders and 5s were, well, not. I never met his code 5s but I sure met plenty of his code 4s over the years, which were as unfriendly and dangerous as any wild cattle, maybe more so, as they didn't seem to have any fear of humans, just plain cunning.

Even after we took on Glen Florrie and started mustering the cattle in with helicopters, bull wagons and horses, rather than trapping, these code 4s still made themselves known. I was flying passenger in the mustering helicopter as a kid (apparently I weighed about as much as a water bottle) when we cleared a holding paddock one day and watched a code 4 cow remain undaunted by the flying machine that pestered her; instead she did her best to hook the chopper skids with her horns. Talk about attitude. Where they were most trouble, though, was in the close confines of the cattle yards. When you stepped into the pen with a code 4, in pretty short order they would have you climbing the fence. 'Dancing the top rail', as it became known, was a common occurrence in the early days and for many years to follow.

My parents took over Glen Florrie in 1993 with the goal of establishing their own herd of breeding cows. It was a slow process. In the first year, we branded seven calves as our own, the progeny of the resident cull cows, some of which we took on as breeders in a bid to raise numbers. The legacy of the code 4s' temperament was destined to live on for quite a few years to come.

Shifting away from Grandad's trapping method towards mustering with helicopters and bull wagons had its challenges. The cattle weren't used to this style of handling and due to Glen Florrie's location and size, there were a significant number of feral cattle turning up out of the hills, which hadn't had any handling at all. Glen Florrie adjoins the unfenced Barlee Range Nature Reserve whose hills and gorges are home to a seemingly endless number of feral cattle. These are wild cattle who have never been handled by humans, or at least not successfully; they're also known as cleanskins due to their lack of ear marks or brands. They are the remnants of early mobs of shorthorns which were introduced into the pastoral country to run alongside sheep in the late 1800s. Their presence is a testament to their ability to survive. They are tough, temperamental, highly fertile, predominantly sharp horned and, well, usually not very pretty. The wild bulls, also known as scrubbers, scrub bulls or dustybacks, due to their penchant for dousing themselves in dirt, often wander out of the hills to infiltrate the domesticated herds. They fight the high-value herd bulls and leave their mark in the resulting undesirable progeny when they win. As frustrating as it can be to find the interlopers amongst a beautiful line of breeders, these feral cattle, and the bulls in particular, provide much excitement at mustering time, as they do their best to escape back into the hills. Once in the yards, any semblance of civility they may have shown usually vanishes as they experience capture for the first time.

Ironically, with most attention focused on the feral bulls, cows can often prove to be the more dangerous animal, and can catch people unawares. This proved true during a muster in 1994, when my brother was nine. We were on the homeward stretch of a muster, with only a few kilometres left to go before we reached the homestead cattle yards. Murray had a beautiful old grey pony called Marley. She had been in the family for most of her 24 years, teaching generations of our extended family during her time.

On this day, while I was riding shotgun in the bull wagon with Dad, a mob of feral cattle was brought out of the river by the helicopter for us to guide into the coacher mob. Coachers are the first mob of cattle that are put together early in the day; they usually settle subsequent fresh cattle as these are brought in during the muster and the mob moves towards the yards. In this fresh mob we were directing towards the coachers, there was a stark-white feral cow with wickedly sharp curved horns. Taking no notice of the coachers, the crew that was tending them, or even the rest of her own small mob, this cow picked out a target and charged headlong at Murray and Marley. Dad couldn't get between them with the bull wagon in time to block her charge and she slammed into the side of Marley with a vicious twist of her horns. Uncle Jim, who was driving a ute we called the Enterprise, managed to get between Murray, who had fallen off Marley, and the cow. As Murray crawled onto the back of the ute with blood running down the leg of his jeans from a ten-centimetre gash in his calf muscle, another family friend leant down from her horse and grabbed Marley's reins to lead her away from the mob. Though Marley had sustained injuries to her flank during the first charge, it was the second that proved her undoing. As she was being led down the road ahead of the mob towards home and out of harm's way, the same cow came back out of the mob to finish what she started. Unable to dodge the unexpected charge while already injured, and with no vehicles close enough to intercept, Marley was gored again in the flank. We did our best to patch her together with what we had on hand and carefully put her in the float to take her home to the back lawn for more treatment, but the shock from the injury took its toll.

Murray and I had our beds outside on the verandah at the time and, during the night, after Murray's leg had been tended to and we had fallen asleep, my parents saw Marley walk around to where my brother slept and say a silent goodbye before she found her final resting place on the lawn.

Though station work has its dangers, our parents always encouraged us to be involved and I'm glad they did. We received our fair share of bumps and bruises along the way but the responsibilities and lessons we learnt have been invaluable in the ensuing years.

*

There was a turning point a few years after my parents took over when the behaviour of our cattle during round-up started to noticeably improve. We continued to receive cattle from Thangoo but we were slowly building our own breeder herd alongside them. The extra handling our cattle received during mustering by gathering and droving them rather than trapping with a quick release out of the yards was improving their manners. Mum played a big part in the education of our cattle during mustering. She had always maintained her love of horses and on every breeder muster, she would be out steadying the lead of the mob on her faithful chestnut horse, Elita. The smart old mare would zigzag across the road, ears back and tail flicking at any animal who tried to walk up level with her, setting the pace while Mum had her nose buried in a book. I would do much the same thing on my pony, Taffy, at the tail of the mob on most musters. Taffy was a sassy little mare who had me dodging teeth when I tightened the girth and watching my toes for an errant hoof. No bigger than the cattle, she was so well rounded in the belly, she earnt herself the nicknames Watermelon Horse and Fat Pony from much-loved local legend Rossy Rotor, our mustering pilot.

Mustering is one of the most exciting events on a cattle station. Each property has a different program and some properties do two laps a year, but the purpose is the same. During a muster, the cattle are gathered together from an area and yarded up into either permanent or portable yards. From there, they are drafted (sorted), with sale cattle being sent direct to market or moved to a holding paddock to be sold later. We were building our herd up with Brahmans, which are notorious scavengers, chewing on almost everything, including old bones and carcases when they are chasing phosphorus, a mineral Australia is widely deficient in. We had to vaccinate these cattle for botulism, a naturally occurring toxic bacteria in the soil that can be picked up while chewing on bones and may prove fatal. While building up our numbers early on, we didn't cull many breeding cows. As long as they were producing a calf, they were retained, even most of the code 4s we had inherited. Calves and cleanskins were ear-marked and fire-branded for each area until we had covered most of the property. Some areas of the station ran lower numbers of stock so it could only be mustered every three years or so until the numbers built up and it became viable to do it more frequently. These musters were the ones everyone wanted to be involved in, because they usually produced scrubbers galore.

I still remember the buzz of excitement that arrived with the helicopter flying in just on dusk the night before a muster. The men would be doing last-minute prep work to the bull wagons under the workshop lights while Murray and I raced up to the airstrip to watch the helicopter set down. We had a game we played each time, taking bets with each other on which part of the chopper would stop spinning first, the main blades overhead or the tail rotor. Considering, as we learnt later, that both rotors are interconnected and there would have been a serious issue if they had in fact stopped at different times, there was never a conclusive winner, but we had fun debating. As Glen Florrie manager now, I still feel that childhood buzz, but it is dulled somewhat by the weight of responsibility for making sure everything is organised and prepped. There's now an underlying anxiety as I wonder just what might go wrong this time. We kids didn't know how good we had it.

The sound of the generator starting at 4.30 am was our cue to get up. Mum would have breakfast cooking and the makings of her famous mustering sandwiches laid out on the island bench. Last-minute jobs were undertaken, horses fed a quick breakfast and two-way radios distributed. At first light, the familiar whine of the chopper engine being turned over and the distinctive whup-whup of the long blades beginning to spin signalled the official start of the muster, as the chopper lifted off to head out looking for cattle and we followed in our respective vehicles, with the horses in tow.

Despite the hustle and bustle of the morning, mustering on a station is often a case of 'hurry up and wait', as you gather in a clearing where the first of the cattle are predicted to arrive. Rossy's familiar call of 'Motorcar, motorcar,' over the radio was the signal we were all waiting for. The day's fun had finally started. The first mob that was picked up was usually the trickiest. The cattle were fresh and you didn't have a coacher mob already settled to run them into. Sometimes, with a lot of quick thinking and skilled manoeuvring, the situation could be brought under control. Sometimes it couldn't, with most, if not all, the cattle scattering and disappearing back into the scrub before we could get a handle on them. The turning point came one muster as we waited on a clear flat area in our bull wagons (Suzukis for us kids and short-wheel-base Toyotas for the others, apart from Mum who always saddled up her horse). Rossy's call came in. He had our first mob and they were heading towards us at pace. Our job in the buggies was to circle the mob and steady them to a stop, if we could. Mum and anyone else on horseback generally waited until the situation was a bit more under control before they joined us.

The rule was to all travel in the same direction and follow the tail of the vehicle in front of us as we 'ringed' the cattle. This system is tried and tested, possibly explaining where the Australian term 'ringers' comes from. Every gap was covered by a vehicle passing it or coming towards it, every vehicle had someone backing them up in case any cattle tried to escape through the gap behind. This also reduced chances

Rossy Rotor and Dad discussing plans while Murray and I suss out his helicopter with a family friend.

of a collision between vehicles and avoided 'tooth-pasting', a definite no-no in mustering where two vehicles are going after the same animal from different sides, with the undesired effect of making the animal run faster as it aims for the closing gap.

This time, though, as we braced for chaos, the cattle pulled up to a stop and stared at us like they didn't know what all the fuss was about. My mouth was actually hanging open in surprise, as we sat there with our vehicles idling away, our earlier hype now feeling like overkill. It was such a momentous occasion for Glen Florrie, even the chopper pilot made comment on it. And our cattle only continued to improve.

Dad started putting in small 'night' paddocks at our main mustering points so we had somewhere to release our breeder cows after we had drafted and vaccinated them and recorded their details. This kept them close by, freed up yard space as we marked their calves out to them and allowed for better mothering-up rates, with cows and calves being reunited more easily. For a few days they would graze in the paddock, which had till then been kept empty to preserve feed, then the gate would be opened back to the larger area. For the yard sites where we didn't have night paddocks, as we called them, the cows would be held in the yards until the calves had been mixed back in, then let out of the yards with a few ground crew to steady them up until the majority appeared to be paired up again. This reinforcing of manners, blocking up when asked, not just disappearing in a cloud of dust as some were wont to do, calf be damned, was a big step in the right direction in the educating of our cattle.

*

The most exciting place to be in a muster was with Dad, riding passenger in his bull wagon. I jumped in every chance I could, but once I was needed in my own buggy as part of the crew, these opportunities were limited. When I broke my collarbone at ten and couldn't drive, I got the chance to ride shotgun with Dad again and it was worth the gritted teeth as we bounced over the rough country. Fitted out with a V8 engine and automatic gear box, it was a mean machine. It had a bench seat where Dad's red heeler, imaginatively named Dog, and I would strap in. It was a hard call as to which side of the seat was safer. On the inside you had to dodge Dad's flying elbow as he raced around trees and through creeks after cattle. But it offered you more protection from copping a stinging branch to the cheek, which you risked if you sat on the outside seat. You also had to avoid the heat from the second radiator that had been added where the passenger door would have been. Dad's red heeler and I usually ended up huddled in the middle, watching the drama unfold around us in a fast-paced blur. Though it was an adrenalin rush of excitement, Dad's expert driving made it one of the safest places to be. Pants full of sticks and prickles were just part of the experience.

*

As our herd grew and the steady stream of cattle from Thangoo slowed, we purchased a small Brahman stud herd from Queensland to breed our own bulls with, and a line of pregnant shorthorn cows to build up our breeder numbers. These shorthorns were a vastly different animal to the shorthorn feral cattle that lived in our hills. Though we were aiming for a predominantly Brahman-based mob, the pregnant cows were a quick means of boosting our numbers. In the early days, we couldn't afford to be too fussy. Any female bovine that passed through the yards with even a hint of the Brahman hump or floppy ears was marked as a breeder. As soon as we had our baseline of breeders, we could start culling for temperament. The rule was made, if Mum and I couldn't handle them in the yards, they were sold. We could finally start weeding out the code 4s' ongoing influence.

I'm not sure our neighbours shared our enthusiasm for the Brahman breed, which scaled the hills that had previously provided a boundary between properties like goats. Fencing on properties this size is no small feat and, where possible, mountain ranges are used as a reasonably effective barrier. I think of Brahmans as the thoroughbreds of the cattle world: athletic, smart and sensitive. But they handled the heat well, their excess skin acting like a large radiator to help cool them down, as did their ability to sweat rather than pant. If any breed could thrive on Glen Florrie's rocky terrain, it was these beautiful animals.

Mum's love of numbers led us to introduce an individual recording system for our cattle, a far cry from the tally system that got jotted down in an old pocket-sized notebook. Her new recording system allowed us to keep track of a cow's calving status, its weight (once we installed scales), and any notes pertaining to each individual animal. It was time-consuming to an extent, with technology struggling in the dusty yards, but it was Mum's pet project and her enthusiasm couldn't be dimmed. It's a system we still use today, though it has evolved over the years as technology and our management systems have changed and improved.

The skills and lessons we learnt throughout our childhood held us in good stead as we tackled new challenges in life. Pulling windmills, learning bush mechanics, caring for all kinds of animals and feeling the weight of responsibility – our parents did an incredible job of setting us up well for the future. Looking back now, it's hard to say how our childhood could have been better.

Chapter Four

The Next Generation

'Just because you grow up on a farm doesn't mean
you know how to manage one.'
— Charles Massy, regeneration expert

Murray left school at the end of Year 11, and lived in Perth, working at a farm supplies shop for a short stint, before moving back up to the station to help our parents run the property. In 2004, during my final year at Narrogin Ag College, we purchased a farm 1200 kilometres south of Glen Florrie and my parents made the difficult decision to end their marriage but continue running the business together. Dad moved part-time to the farm and continued running the trucking enterprise, though mostly shifting our own cattle, while Murray stepped up as manager at Glen Florrie with Mum and Dad's continued guidance. The new farm was used mostly as another paddock of the station and provided a relief valve during dry times. Set up with well-established tagastaste (lucerne) paddocks across a large portion of it, the farm provided good forage that our cattle adapted to well.

It was around this time at a New Year's party at Bremer Bay on the south coast of Western Australia that Murray met the love of his life, Adele. She was the cousin of one of his best mates, and it was a case of love at first sight. At least, it was for Murray. Del was only exposed to the off-duty side of him at those times when he was having short breaks in Perth, catching up with his mates over some rum and computer games. But in July 2006 she visited the station to complete her farm placement prac for the Veterinary degree she was doing and came to see the other side of him – a mature, sensible young man, competent and capable in his role as station manager. Juggling a long-distance relationship was no easy feat, but they made it work.

*

Meanwhile, I had briefly attended the Muresk Institute in 2005 in pursuit of an Agribusiness degree before deciding that moving full-time back to the station was the right plan for me. I took my place as Murray's right-hand woman as well as Mum's offsider around the house and in the office. The station budget was Murray's forte, with his talent for numbers, while I preferred actuals over projections, learning to do the quarterly BAS and reconciling accounts via our computer program. I always joke that when Murray is doing paddock carting in the truck, he'll be working out feed rations and percentages of expected weight gain. Meanwhile, I'll be driving along wondering what's for dinner. Priorities and all.

I loved the station cooking and gardening side of the property, though as a kid I would gripe about being stuck in the kitchen helping Mum with dinner while the boys were all out telling stories of the day's adventures. Mum and I and anyone else available spent many a day in the lead-up to musters cooking up a storm with Slim Dusty playing in the background. We put large numbers of slices, cakes, biscuits and quiches through the oven, always doubling the recipes to make them go a little further with the hungry crew. We had an old stainless-steel hospital oven, large but temperamental, even on her good days. If you had to fire her up, you made sure you had plenty to go in to make the effort of warming her up worthwhile. The thermostat was long gone, along with a fair bit of her insulation and she would undoubtedly have a 'slow day' the night before mustering when we were trying to feed the mustering crowd a big meal of roast beef early so they could head to bed.

Mum became known for her great mustering sandwiches and even now, her sandwich system holds strong and is loved by all. The extra little touches like patting the tinned beetroot dry with paper towel to stop the bread going soggy and customising the sandwiches to each person's preferences took them to the next level. I'm not sure if it's because you are usually starving by lunch after the early start or the jostling they get during the ride in the tucker wagon, but mustering sandwiches are always the best.

Murray and I also spent stints working at the farm, in between busy times at the station. I couldn't get over the novelty of actually being able to see the whole of the property from one vantage point. Paddocks were small enough that you could clear them in an hour. What you can achieve on a farm is so different to a station, with its vast paddocks and open, unfenced areas. Dad often drew the short straw and would do Christmas at the station while Murray and I had a 'break' at the farm, putting in new fences and managing the cattle while Mum took the opportunity to travel.

*

Taking on the management of Glen Florrie was a big ask of someone so young, but Murray stepped up to the challenge. With a brain for technology, he was keen to start utilising more solar-powered pumps to water our cattle rather than relying solely on windmills. We can often get what's known as 'wind droughts', when there isn't a breath of breeze for weeks at a time, rendering windmills useless and leading to many hours spent driving between water points and restarting pumps. What is quite rare in our area is 'sun droughts', though you can have a string of overcast days which might cause a few water shortages in your solar-powered pumps, but not as often. What Murray aimed for was a mix of both, with windmills and solar pumps scattered alternately across the property, all within a five-kilometre radius of the next water point. This allowed for a back-up for cattle to move to the next water and reduced the chances of stock perishing. Even with this infrastructure in place, there were still times when water couldn't keep up with the stock load, for a range of reasons, and many a night was spent, especially over the hot summer months, sleeping in a swag on the back of the ute while waiting for a tank to refill from the generator you had to start. Down the track, as pumping systems became more efficient and we developed more watering points to spread cattle on to, these late-night camp-outs became less frequent.

We also invested in a telemetry system that allowed us to remotely monitor our main waters from the homestead and address issues as they happened, like a pump stopping or a trough starting to leak. We weighed up the expense against the time saved travelling hundreds of extra kilometres each week to check waters. The single biggest pressure and responsibility of summer on the station was and still is maintaining water to the livestock.

*

Though Dad's preference was bull wagons, Murray started utilising two-wheel motorbikes for mustering and their versatility couldn't be argued with. They had more endurance than a horse and more manoeuvrability than a bull wagon. The chopper would call bikes out to follow a mob of cattle into the coachers, known as tailing. With a pack strapped on their back for water and a few snacks stuffed in their pockets, the bike riders often wouldn't be back at the tucker wagon until late in the muster. Lunch would be packed in with the pilot when he landed for fuel, and dropped down to the weary riders from above. Meanwhile, buggy drivers and horse riders would enjoy a nice nap in the warm winter sun as we waited for our first coachers to arrive. I tried joining the two-wheel club one year, purchasing a 230cc motorbike. We lowered the bike's suspension so my legs could reach the ground and support me if I hit a buffel-grass clump. The lowered suspension didn't add to the comfort level on the day I headed out and down to the river. As I bounced over large river stones and navigated my way under low-hanging branches and around tea-tree saplings with not a cow in sight, I heard the call come through over the radio from the pilot: 'Just keep an eye out down there on those bikes, you've got a couple of scrub bulls heading back towards you.'

I didn't even wait to see them, I just turned tail and started bouncing my way back along the river the way we had come. I could be brave when I faced off with a bull in a vehicle that weighed more than they did, but put me on a two-wheel bike and I went to water. First chance I had to swap back into my buggy saw me graciously handing my precious bike over to one of the other crew who was keen to ride it. I take my hat off to those who are brave enough to face wild cattle with nothing but skill and tyres, but it sure ain't me. My forte was the bull wagon and, over the years, I became quite proficient in it. I often griped that I needed a younger sibling to pass the mantle to, as Murray did to me, so I could step down from the high-pressure role, but it was also a personal point of pride that not many bulls were able to escape me. In later years, we added a catching arm to my buggy, allowing me to drive alongside a bull and trap him essentially in a headlock. This was a quick, efficient and safer method than the traditional rolling onto the ground, and I could have the bull safely secured to a tree for later retrieval in a matter of minutes.

Murray and I had a few learning curves along the way as we tackled musters without Dad on hand. One time we were mustering a water point called Toms, out to our west, where we had a nice line of breeders established. It also had a not-so-nice line of scrub bulls which would turn up periodically, and on this particular muster we picked up plenty. Contrary to our expectations, the muster went smoothly and soon we had a yard of around 500 head of cattle, with no escapees, breakdowns or mishaps. One for the record books. Feeling quite chuffed with ourselves, as we were a young crew tackling a big job, with Mum being the only person there over 22 years of age, we got the cattle drafted, the cows and calves bushed, and prepared to start shifting the rest to the homestead yards to be readied for sale.

That's when the trouble started. Our ever reliable Scania had a broken compressor so she remained parked up in the shed while we tried cranking up the other old truck on hand, to no avail. With Dad not due back at the station for a few days, we decided on another plan to get the cattle home. We had a flat-top trailer with stock gates on it which we could pull behind a vehicle without needing a compressor to release the brakes, allowing us to at least get about thirty head home at a time. We hooked the forty-foot trailer on behind the bull wagon manned by Koro, a friend I met during my short stint at college, then hooked the ute on with a chain in front of that. Between the two vehicles we figured we had enough power to get the trailer and cattle over the hills that stood between us and home. We were right, we had plenty of power. What we lacked was brakes.

Our driveway is 88 kilometres of winding gravel road, with hills and sharp bends scattered along it. There is one corner in particular, aptly named Danger Bend after the homemade warning sign that precedes it, where the road comes out of the hills before turning sharply with a three-metre drop off the outside. After hitting the final climb with enough pace to clear it, Murray guided the ute towards the bend, coasting along steady in second gear. I was in the passenger seat, subconsciously stamping my foot against the floor as my instincts told me we needed to slow down further. But Murray was in the driver's seat and therefore in the best place to feel the weight of the load as we drew near the corner but he was finding it hard to judge with the extra vehicle in between. As we entered the turn, things started to go awry. With too much momentum and weight and not enough pull to swing it around the sharp bend, the trailer slowly toppled over the edge. As the buggy started to be pulled sideways, Koro sensibly bailed out and we all watched on in disbelief as the crate tipped onto its side and the cattle enclosed stepped out unharmed and trotted down into the river. Of course, we had loaded the trailer full of scrub bulls and sappy mickeys (young bulls), the best sale cattle from the muster, and as grateful as we were that they weren't injured, it was hard to watch the cattle disappear back out of reach.

Hindsight is a wonderful thing but so is experience. Both buggy and ute were completely undamaged, aside from a twisted hitch where the trailer had been hooked onto the back so we were never in harm's way. But it still hit Murray hard, knowing that it could have ended badly. Dad said, when he heard of our dramas, 'I could have told you that wouldn't work,' and I'm sure he could have, but it was an experience we needed.

*

With a focus on fertility, Murray introduced the practice of pulling weaners off their mothers when we mustered our breeders and holding the young cattle in a small paddock until they learnt to manage away from mum. Many cows will naturally wean a calf once it's old enough, but quite a few can't or don't. It's heartbreaking to watch a big sappy weaner drinking off a cow while her next calf struggles to get enough milk to thrive. Pulling the weaners off also acted as a trigger for many of the cows to cycle again. Ideally, with a gestation of nine months, they would be getting back in calf before this point, when their current calf was about three months old. In most cases, they are triggered to cycle by a flush of feed after decent rain as their body condition improves or, if that doesn't happen, by their weaner being taken off them. Removing a calf or weaner off a cow and allowing her to reabsorb that milk can be equivalent to feeding her two kilos of grain a day. It allows the cow to have a break in between raising calves to recover and maintain decent body condition, also known as body score condition.

Following on from the basics I learnt at ag college, we hosted a small school at Glen Florrie to learn how to pregnancy test cattle. Murray gave it a go but after calling an eight-months pregnant cow 'empty' (the term used for not in calf) and an empty cow pregnant, he decided his skills lay in other areas. Mum did just enough to keep her hand in over the next few years, so to speak, while I practised the technique till I was confident enough to add it to our management practices. Suddenly we didn't have to guess if a cow was producing calves or not purely from visual observation, which can be very deceptive unless the cow is 'springing', or about to calve. With a simple exam, I could establish a pregnancy or lack of it. Almost immediately we saw the improvement in our calving rates, as 'free loaders' or what we called 'career cows', who were perpetually empty, were identified and culled (selected to be sold) from the herd. In a business where margins are low and every animal has to be productive, these girls weren't pulling their weight so they would be sold.

Although there are benefits to the management practice of controlled mating where bulls are only run with the cows for a short period of time – for example, a smaller calving window and cows calving down at the ideal time of year for feed availability – it requires a significant amount of infrastructure to achieve this. Murray had completed a Grazing for Profit course run by Resource Consulting Services and was keen to implement this mating practice on Glen Florrie. But our mustering lap took too long, and we didn't have time to do a second round to pull the bulls back out again. And, even if we did, there were still too many mickeys and scrubbers that were being missed during the musters who would be more than happy to handle the job in the absence of our herd bulls. It was a great goal but one that wasn't yet achievable on the station. Where it was much more achievable was on our farm, with its numerous paddocks and ease of stock movement, and Murray was able to establish it there with our stud cattle in later years.

At this point, our weaners weren't receiving any extra handling beyond what was absolutely necessary. We didn't realise the importance of educating or training them; our main focus was on separating them from their mothers and relocating them out to the other side of the property so heifers (young females who haven't had a calf yet) couldn't breed back to their fathers. It wasn't without its hiccups. I remember one particular day when we had finished mustering an area and had a mob of marked weaners in the homestead yards. We had constructed a five-kilometre-long laneway between our house yards and our holding paddocks the previous summer, which we now used for shifting cattle between the two. When Murray and I set out to take this young mob of 400 or so weaners into the laneway, they were stressed, scared, unprepared and inclined to run. We were unprepared too, as it turned out. We let the weaners out of the yards into an open area that led to the start of the laneway and they scattered like marbles on a glass tabletop. Murray and I tore around on bikes with no hope of keeping the mob together, trying only to get the lead of the mob headed towards the laneway in the hope the tail might follow. Instead, they dispersed at speed in three different directions, all the wrong way. This is also known as 'blowing' and we had well and truly 'blown' this mob. We ended up with spooked weaners in three different paddocks and in multiple different mobs. Hardly ideal. I pulled up on the bike, pushed my hat back in exasperation and thought, 'There must be an easier way.'

*

Murray and Adele's long-distance relationship had survived the test of time. Adele graduated university with her Veterinary degree and they became engaged in March 2011, while enjoying a holiday cruise with friends. A few months later, after securing a job in Queensland, Del moved interstate for two years. Once he finished the season at the station, Murray joined her at Christmas for six months while he continued to make plans and budgets for the business. Luckily, timely summer rain made this possible, after being in very short supply for the previous two years.

Glen Florrie had suffered a terrible year in 2010, when feed dried off quickly despite 2009's decent summer rain, resulting in a large number of cattle being shifted down to our farm and onto agistment country we secured nearby. As we mustered, we were pulling all the calves off the cows to help them get through, shifting the babies home in a small truck we called Fugly. This was an achievement in itself, with the calves startling easily and piling up numerous times during the trip till they found their feet. We would unload at the yards and start the long process of getting them drinking on a bottle. As the days progressed, we would slowly shift the early adopters over to receiving their milk from a bar feeder while we persevered with the non-conformers.

That year, we put over 200 calves on milk, compared to a 'normal' year of maybe ten. We would separate them into different mobs depending on their size and age so they received their specific milk requirements. Then we would feed them every morning in batches of twelve: ten calves across two bar feeders with two on bottles till the whole mob was done. With seemingly no break in between, we would then start prepping for the afternoon meal.

These weren't the only calves we were looking after. It was only the smallest that received milk, with the larger calves and weaners being drafted into mobs, again according to size, age and condition. They were fed a mix of pellets and quality oaten hay until they were able to survive independently on grass and be sent south to the farm. We were fortunate that the sharp dry spell was broken by decent rain in January 2011 and many of the breeders we had sent south on agistment were able to come home with the flush of feed. It was a year we were glad to see the back of.

Murray and Adele were married in the beautiful town of York, west of Perth, surrounded by friends and family in late 2012. I was honoured to stand next to Murray as his 'best man', my black dress with its royal-blue sash mirroring the groomsmen's handsome attire. Del looked absolutely stunning in a beautiful lace wedding gown, with her lovely bridesmaids in dark purple dresses alongside. Not long after, Del returned to Queensland to continue her Veterinary placement while Murray stayed on running the station.

Chapter Five

The Dog World

'Hands off the handlebars.'
– Wayne Woods, dog handler

My journey into the working-dog world wasn't without its bumps and bruises. Even though I had always had a dog by my side, I didn't know the value of a good working dog. Dad preferred red heelers, who would follow him around the cattle yards, 'helping' with pen-up. Dad only ever had one at a time but over the years he had a few who all worked in a similar manner. They would pressure the cattle with heel bite and bark when they felt brave, or hide behind us and trip us up when they didn't. One of Dad's heelers loved waiting outside the headbale (also known as a cattle crush, where you hold an animal steady while you mark or treat them) to greet the cattle as they were let out, spinning around in a quick twirl and barking at them as they fled. Entertaining antics to watch, perhaps, but not good for the cattle, as Mum often pointed out in exasperation.

As far as I knew, heelers were the only working dogs worth having on a cattle station, so after I left school, I picked up my own little pup. Leah was a lovely dog, who had the typical Australian cattle dog traits of chasing heels, barking at stock and biting people. My dog-training skills extended to teaching her a couple of tricks – like playing dead when I pretended to shoot her with a bang (though she often believed my aim was off) and picking up objects with a 'look' command until she lucked on the item I wanted and proudly brought it over. A very handy trick for those just-out-of-reach things and one I really need to teach a member of my crew now. But that was the extent of my dog-training ability. I also nursed a sneaking suspicion that although Leah had some very handy traits like shaking off kicks to the head as only an Australian cattle dog can and the keenness to back it up, the cattle dog's work style was lacking in some way.

*

The first time I glimpsed the potential of a good working dog was during a trip to New Zealand in my early twenties. I had gone across with my boyfriend at the time for Christmas with his family, and we took the opportunity to do a road trip around the islands. Meeting a range of handlers on different farms opened my eyes to a whole world I hadn't consciously realised existed. At one point, we pulled up on the side of the road to watch a man standing on top of a high hill direct his dogs around the paddock as they herded the sheep within it, using only a series of seemingly indistinguishable whistles. I was amazed at how well he could orchestrate the situation, controlling all those minds with seemingly minimal effort. To this day, I still think folk in New Zealand are in a league of their own when it comes to working dogs – one I can only aspire to.

Seeing the huntaways and heading dogs that operated in New Zealand sparked my interest in working dogs, so when the opportunity arose to attend a Neil McDonald Advanced Livestock and Working Dog School early in 2013, I jumped at it. Neil McDonald is a renowned dog trainer, teaching schools across Australia for over 30 years. Realising the importance of good stock handling, his schools teach you more than just how to work a dog, they also teach you how to handle livestock. Something I hadn't appreciated at all. Turns out just because you have been doing something for twenty years, doesn't mean you are any good at it.

I often say I went to my first dog school with no dogs and knowing I knew nothing about them. This isn't really stretching the truth. What I did know was that Leah probably wasn't going to fit the bill, so I decided to leave her at home as I headed to Geraldton, which as it turns out, was wise. There were no heelers at the school and I soon learnt why as I appreciated for the first time the natural skill and stock sense of the Australian kelpie.

Anyone who has done one of Neil's schools will attest that they are an overload of information, covering not just dog training and stock movements but also stock psychology, human psychology, farm management, working-dog history, OHS and welfare considerations, peppered throughout with colourful stories from Neil's experiences and often entertaining demonstrations. By the end of the third day, you feel mentally and emotionally exhausted, and slightly shell shocked to boot. Neil's schools have something for every skill and experience level and there is more to learn than one can absorb in a single hit. Many times over the years I have had 'lightbulb' moments when the next piece of the puzzle suddenly makes sense, but I couldn't fully grasp or understand what Neil was trying to teach until I had the previous practice well established. And full credit to Neil, he never stops learning either, attending other trainers' clinics to learn new skills and passing on techniques he's learnt as he travels across Australia educating both people and dogs.

The upfront cost of the school did raise questions with my family, mainly from my dad who didn't see why I would need to attend a school to learn to handle stock I had been around most of my life. But a very generous offer from a close friend of a free kelpie pup called Zen if I attended tipped the scales in my favour. I had no idea how pivotal to my life these next few days would turn out to be.

From the first day of the school, I was hooked. What really cemented it for me was seeing the dynamic of Neil's dog camp and the rapport he had with each of the eighteen dogs he had tied up along a gang chain in the shade by a creek, near the truck where he camped. They were all evenly spaced on short tethers so they couldn't get tangled around each other or anything else. They had bright eyes and happy natures, excited beyond belief to hear Neil's quad bike approach. For dogs who were spending the majority of the day and night tied up, they were incredibly 'settled' in the head. These were dogs that had been on the chain all day, let off in the morning for a quick drink, feed and toilet break, then tied back up again until that evening, and yet there was no sulking back to the chain when called (a practice Leah had down to a fine art, if I ever had the audacity to suggest she go on a rope), no whining or complaining. They were all happy. Happier, of course, if they were one of the select few taken out for a job or to 'stooge' (be a working dog) for the participants at school.

Our heelers were what Neil calls 'Gold Coaster dogs', rarely ever tied up and allowed to run around doing as they pleased any time of the day. You can usually pick a Gold Coaster at a dog school as soon as the owner tries to do a task with it. The dog will spend its time introducing itself to the other dogs, smelling and marking scents, taking in the new surroundings and generally ignoring the (by now quite embarrassed) owner who is trying to get on with the job at hand. There are always exceptions, of course, but generally, a dog that is free to do as it pleases at home is inclined to do as it pleases at a school. Suddenly, all the new and unfamiliar scents and dogs are far more interesting than working a few old sheep.

I have seen dogs who are tied up or caged permanently, never getting a chance to run around to expend some of that energy and miserable because of it, which is cruel and unnecessary. What I learnt at Neil's school was it is necessary to keep dogs tied up, for a range of reasons, but that there is a kind way to do it. Keeping a dog restrained, kennelled or closely supervised when it's not working keeps it fresh in the mind, keen to do the job at hand and also, most importantly, alive. You don't often hear of a kennel being run over, but everyone seems to know of a dog that didn't make it back out from under a wheel while running around loose. And nothing adds a bit of tension to neighbourly relations like an unrestrained working dog (or pet for that matter) paying an uninvited visit to stock on the wrong side of the fence. After seeing Neil's happy camp and the work ethic and dedication of his dogs, I knew he was right.

As I helped Neil pack up his tents at the end of day three, I asked him for a favour. I knew this was something that

I wanted to do, that I had found what I needed in my life without even realising it was missing. I wanted to experience the rapport I had witnessed between Neil and his dogs and the end result of educated, calm stock. So I asked Neil to put together a going team of dogs for me, sight unseen. And my journey into the world of working dogs began.

Chapter Six

Student First, Teacher Second

**'When you bite off more than you can chew,
just learn to chew harder.'**

— A very wise person

There are many different ways to get started with a team of dogs. You might take on a young pup with the plan to learn with them. Maybe with good luck you get an older semi-retired dog who can show you the ropes, who's tolerant of the many rookie mistakes and unintended offences you are destined to make. Or you could be like me and jump in at the deep end, by purchasing four 'going' dogs (dogs already working stock with commands) and a dog trailer on the other side of Australia, and organising a road trip with your sister-in-law to bring them all home.

As luck would have it, my foray into working dogs coincided nicely with Adele's move home from Queensland. Though Neil at first had reservations about whether I would follow through with my plan of getting a team of dogs, I convinced him I was committed, and a few months after the school, he found me an already established team of four female kelpies for sale. Taking his word that they would suit what I needed, with no idea of their style, history or anything else, I transferred the money, found a second-hand dog trailer for sale in the general vicinity and bought a plane ticket to Bundaberg. Del picked me up from the airport, with the last two years of her life, a kitten, her black Labrador and now me packed into her four-wheel-drive, ready for the long trip home.

Considering the menagerie we had with us even before we picked up my new dogs, we tried to overnight with people we knew rather than land on unprepared strangers. With a spare day up our sleeve before we could collect the dogs, we trekked to Longreach and ticked the Stockman's Hall of Fame off our bucket list. We left our return to Barcaldine a little late in the day and thanks to a decent shower of rain, soon learnt more about the area's lovely black soil than we ever wanted to know. The dirt road changed to mud and the sticky black clay built up around the tyres until we couldn't drive any further, resulting in the two of us, barefoot and drenched from the rain, trying to scrape the mud clear with a wheel brace and a screwdriver. I never thought I'd be grateful for our slippery red-soil country till that night.

The next day, after picking up my new dog trailer from Ilfracombe near Longreach, we arrived at the farm where my new team of dogs awaited. I had purchased a beautiful red-and-tan girl called Diddy, older than the others and striking in her almost masculine build and solid head. There were two black-and-tan kelpies – Ang, distinctive with her pointed ears and a lovely dark tinge to her tan; and Flora, pale tan stark against her black coat, framing floppy ears and wary eyes. The last was Julia, half-sister to Ang and aptly named after the prime minister of the time with her solid red coat.

As we drove away with the dogs safely tucked in the trailer, I sat clutching a scrap of notepaper with four names scrawled on it, wondering belatedly just what I had gotten myself into. I'm sure Del was wondering the same thing.

*

As it turned out, while we headed towards Katherine in the Northern Territory, Neil McDonald was handling some cattle on a property nearby in preparation for another training school the following week. Considering how long it had been since Del had last seen Murray, I appreciated that she agreed to the delay in our trip while I caught up with Neil. When we arrived, Neil was moving a mob of cattle through the yards with his dogs and, after introducing us to the property owners, he invited me to bring out my new dogs for a look.

I was full of trepidation. I wasn't sure how to call my dogs or if I even had their names correct at this point, let alone how to ask them to start working stock. The only working dogs I had used prior to this were Neil's stooges at the school I attended and that suddenly seemed like a long time ago.

There are a few aspects of working dogs that seem to defy human logic until it is explained correctly and you can look at it from a dog's perspective. An example of this is when we ask a dog to go in a particular direction. We usually point the way we want them to go because, well, that just makes sense, right? Turns out we are actually telling the dog we want them to go in the opposite direction, because our arm, leg and body language are acting to block the dog from going the way we are pointing. Confusing? It makes sense once you get the hang of it, but try figuring that out with a brand-new dog and an audience of three very experienced dog handlers – Neil and two of his previous students – watching on from the fence line. Feeling the pressure, I crouched down next to Diddy in the middle of the yard and whispered, 'Help me out here girl, I have no idea what I'm doing.'

Once the nerves wore off and Diddy showed me how we did the cattle work, things started to fall into place and those extra few hours under Neil's tutelage set me up well for the rollercoaster ride I was about to begin. One thing I was starting to realise pretty fast, though: I had an uncomfortable number of bad habits to unlearn.

*

Del and I arrived at Glen Florrie just in time for the annual mustering lap to begin. Zen, my kelpie pup, who I had wisely decided didn't need to join us on the road trip, was now a handsome six-month-old with gorgeous dark markings and a trademark goofy expression. Leah accepted the newcomers more easily than I expected and happily tagged along anywhere we went, adding her two bobs' worth when she could.

To say I felt like I was jumping in the deep end would be an understatement. We had another dog called Bruce with us for a few weeks. We had picked him up on the trip across the north from Queensland to the Pilbara, bound for a handler who lived near Geraldton. While my four girls were quite well behaved (mostly), Bruce was a different story.

As Murray loves reminding me, 'Your dogs were good but then there was Bruce. You were trying to convince me that "No, no ... dogs work!" while Bruce, the loose cannon, who paid no attention to anyone, was blowing the poddy calves through fences and chasing your 'roo up the hill. Fun times!'

Yeah, real fun ...

My dog camp started as chains set up under the shade of an old truck bed, conveniently close to the yards but as basic as they come. This lasted for a few months but, as summer drew near, I moved the dogs into some homemade kennels. Divided into five individual cages with partial wooden flooring and a communal water dish running between them, these ground kennels seemed like an upgrade to the Taj Mahal. Out of respect for the other people living at the station, and to protect the dogs from vehicles driving past all the time, the new kennels were parked under the best shade we could find, which was about a kilometre away from the homestead. I had high hopes that the distance might buffer the excessive barking when the dogs were feeling rowdy in the wee hours of the morning, but turns out you need a lot more than one kilometre to achieve that. I don't mind if they have a bit of a bark on occasion and preferably with a reason but, at some point, we need to get some sleep.

One evening after a long day mustering, I thought I'd be smart and beat my dogs at their own game. I secured (turns out badly) one of our two-way radios to the underside of the roof of the kennels so it was protected from any overnight moisture, put the dogs away and headed back to the homestead, feeling smug.

At 2 am, I heard the barking start. Dragging myself out of bed and over to the radio in the dining room, I yelled into the microphone, 'SIT DOWN and BE QUIET!' The silence was glorious and after a few more choice words to keep them in line, I headed back to bed, pretty chuffed with myself.

The next morning, when I arrived at the kennels, all smugness vanished in a hurry when I found a very proud Zen dog sitting next to a very drowned radio, the expensive hand piece floating dismally in his water dish. Lesson learnt: don't leave valuable items within reach of dogs and for the love of all things precious, never, ever, in the pen with the pup.

To top it off, I arrived back at the house for breakfast to find a bleary-eyed ringer regaling the table about forgetting to shut his two-way off the night before and being rudely awoken in the middle of the night with a 'SIT DOWN and BE QUIET!' My idea of remote discipline was shelved for now and this episode notched up as a win to the dogs.

My dog kennels these days have expanded to fifteen individual cages and have been moved under a big, shady gum tree. The old kennels have been refurbished with a new wooden floor and raised up off the ground, out of reach of snakes, termites and ticks. To find a tree that threw a decent amount of shade, we ended up in a low-lying flood area so an evacuation plan for the dogs is in place should the need, or in this case, water arise. We've planted more trees all around the kennels to try to help counter the sun's relentless heat and a lawn is spreading slowly in the area between. The kennels all have a double roof overhead, with shade cloth strategically placed around the mesh cages to limit the sun without hindering the breeze, though the hot wind can be more of a curse than a blessing some days. Every kennel has its own personal swimming pool, which the dog can lie in and drink from if they knock or empty their smaller water bowls. In winter, these tubs double as warm beds with hessian matting or old horse blankets as rugs. This summer we also put a sprinkler system on top of the second roof to try to cool things down further. Everything helps, but at the end of the day, 52 degrees Celsius (and that's in the shade) is never going to be overly pleasant for anyone.

*

Mum has always been a strong supporter of my foray into working dogs, while my brother was a little more sceptical. Considering the great first impression Bruce left, I can't say I blame him. But Murray could see I was passionate about this new venture and offered his unconditional, albeit at times amused, support. When a fresh mob of weaners were due to come in from the mustering yards, he would ask me what my plan was with them, how long would I need them in the yards to educate the cattle to the dogs and then work his plans around them. I, meanwhile, felt like I had no real clue what I was talking about, let alone doing. This wasn't going to change for a while.

When it comes to working weaners, one lesson I learnt very quickly was that if I let my dogs head out onto the job full of pent-up energy, I had to be prepared for them to work more than enthusiastically. My control over my dogs was understandably tenuous when I first got them, which is not to say we don't still have our moments now. But knowing that I had even less hope of controlling the situation while they were fresh, I didn't want to let them out onto our weaners, who needed to settle and be handled with a bit of extra care. Instead we would start our day working with a mob of cull cows who had been drafted out of the breeders to be sold. Cows are usually culled for a few reasons like lack of calves, bad conformation or bad temperament. In most cases, they needed, or could at least handle, a bit of rougher work from my dogs. Once the edge had been taken off the dogs' energy and I had gained some semblance of control, we would head out to start educating the weaners who were softer, more responsive and less confrontational than the older cows.

*

Neil says there are two ways to start educating your cattle to being handled with dogs. You can start by educating your weaners and as the years pass and the next generations are incorporated into your main herd, the youngsters learn at their dam's side and you will eventually end up with a nice herd of educated cattle. Or you can go all in, draw a line and decide that everything is getting educated from now on, cows, weaners, bulls, the lot. You can guess which way I went.

The first six months was a fun game of trial and error. I started using the dogs during our musters. Probably not as effectively as they could have been but we got by. They would all pile into the back of my bull wagon, now upgraded from the small Suzuki to a 'real' buggy, with Leah alongside, and hold on for dear life if I ever had to chase something. They'd help tuck the tail of the mob in or head up front to block the lead if a mob tried to bolt. Sometimes they were successful. Where I felt they had the biggest impact on our cows' manners, though, was in the yards.

One thing I learnt very quickly was our cows were spoilt. Not all of them but more than there should have been. This was mostly due to the way they had been handled previously, learning bad habits and getting away with it. Basically, it was rude.

When drafting a mob of cattle, they need to flow from the larger yards they first enter after they are mustered, known as receiving yards, into progressively smaller yards until they walk up a race or into a round pen to be sorted, vaccinated, preg-tested et cetera. Cows that have been through the yards a time or two soon learn the drill and they either accept it and flow through quietly or they decide they've had enough, and that's when the argument starts. It doesn't take long for the more cunning cows to learn that we are pretty much all bluff and if they run at us, we will try to get out of the way. They also know exactly where the gateway that you are trying to move them through is and will refuse to go through it or they'll run back out quick smart as soon as you move to shut the gate behind them. In most yard-ups, there would be one or two cows that would beat us back through the gate, leaving us with a last pen of stubborn, cunning, cranky cattle refusing to cooperate.

Once I got my dogs, things started to change. When we got to the last yard-up, I'd call the dogs in. This was their sport, their favourite job. It was a no-holds-barred brawl really. When the rebel cows ran back through us, the dogs would be ready. Diddy, Ang, Julia, Flora and Leah (Zen was too young but Leah loved to 'help') would apply full pressure through bark and bites to the nose and front feet. Both very effective ways for a kelpie to earn a cow's respect. There was just one rule. When the cows turned the right way, the dogs had to release the pressure. This was essential. I needed the cows to learn that the smaller yard was where they wanted to be, where they could get relief from the dogs. The skill of knowing when to give relief is not something that comes naturally to all dogs, or even many, but it can be taught, generally with a stop command. Not a command I had over any of my dogs, bar Diddy, at the time (she came conveniently pre-trained) but a call-off can suffice at a pinch. The test came when I walked towards the gates to shut them. If the cows made a move to run back through me and out the gate, I'd step aside and let them. The dogs didn't mind. Eventually, the cows would admit defeat and stand in the smaller yard as the dogs found the water trough and I shut the gate.

It can be a time-consuming task teaching both the dogs and the cattle. Some days we lost half an hour or more working with these cows while they learnt manners and some grudging respect. But the next time they were in the yards, they might not go through the gate the first time, but I can guarantee they didn't take as long to remember the lesson once they saw the dogs again.

*

My father was a reluctant observer of my journey into working a team of dogs. He had always had a dog in his shadow throughout his life, whether it was a hard-biting hanging dog (a dog that bites the nose of a beast and won't let go) during his early years on stations in the Kimberley or a nimble kelpie helping him load sheep in the early days. But he had never had more than one dog at a time and couldn't understand why I needed five.

I really wanted to prove my dogs' worth to Dad (and my own worth as well, in hindsight), and that usually meant, of course, that whenever he was around, things went awry.

The original wooden cattle yards near the homestead at Glen Florrie had slowly been replaced by railway iron posts and conveyer belting, prompted by Dad breaking his foot years earlier when a wooden rail gave out under him while loading cattle. As our breeding herd got larger, the number of cattle we were handling through the yards with each muster increased. Ideally, you need a spacious square yard with minimal obstacles so the weaners can flow easily in a mob as you slowly adjust their flight zone. The purpose of educating cattle is to teach them how to behave calmly and cope with stressful situations. Neil says stress is not knowing when you'll get relief. If you are stranded in the desert with no water, you'd be pretty stressed. But if you know that help is on the way and you'll have relief from your thirst shortly, you'll feel a lot better about the situation. It's the same with cattle. We don't want to protect them from stress while educating them, we want to teach them how to cope with stressful situations in a controlled environment, so that next time they are in a similar situation, they handle it calmly knowing relief is around the corner.

Cattle of all ages can be educated, but older cattle with established habits can make the process longer, slower and more dangerous. Weaners are more pliable, quicker to learn and also safer for dogs to work with purely because of their size. I don't think the importance of educating cattle, especially weaners, can be overstated. It's like taking the time to teach a young horse how to be comfortable under a saddle and subsequently carry and respond to a rider rather than just jumping on and hoping for the best. I mean, that strategy can work too, but you might have a few extra broken bones by the end of it. We need to give animals a chance to learn before we expect them to know.

On this memorable day when things didn't quite go to plan, my intention was to let a fresh mob of 200 weaners out of the yards into the paddock around our airstrip. I was being a little ambitious but I had decided it would be easier to handle the weaners in the paddock than within the restrictions of the limited yard space. Normally, I would have more control over the weaners before I tried to take them out of the yards, teaching them to block up (stop) with the dogs at the very least. But I was feeling confident that we could handle this. So confident in fact, I didn't even have all my dogs on the job. My first mistake.

The paddock I was letting the weaners out into contained the 'lay-down area' where the station machinery was parked. This included the prime mover truck and trailers, which Dad was currently doing maintenance on, only a few hundred metres from the gateway my weaners were about to walk out of.

To say that knowing Dad was watching added a degree of stress to the situation would be an understatement. I had left Diddy secured in the dog trailer, parked about 150 metres away. She was my most experienced dog but she could be inclined to bark and I didn't want the weaners to spook at the noise while we had no fences to hold them in. So I had my other three silent kelpies out with me (no Leah this time) and a friend on hand to help when the gate was swung open to let the weaners out. To be fair to the weaners, they really didn't do anything drastically wrong. They just hadn't been taught yet to respect the dogs enough. As the mob moved further from the yards, spreading widely and paying little heed to the dogs trying to hold them up, I could feel the situation slipping out of control. I could also see Dad looking on with sceptical interest.

I decided to pull out the big guns, in this case Diddy, and hurried over to the dog trailer to let her save the day. Unfortunately, Diddy took off like a firecracker from the trailer, ran to the side of the mob, which she startled with her bark, and next thing I knew, the whole mob took off at a gallop into the far reaches of the paddock, with me hot-footing it after them. My friend headed for the house to grab a bike so we had wheels, while I trailed after the mob on foot, fuming and embarrassed, my dogs valiantly trying to keep in front of the lead.

We eventually got the weaners gathered, settled and tailed back to the yards and through the gate like I originally planned, albeit an hour or so later. In my eyes Diddy was to blame for the weaners rushing. She hit the wrong spot, barked when she didn't need to, and was responsible for the whole blow-up. And she'd had to do it when Dad was watching too, just to confirm his suspicions that this whole dog phase was a mistake. Diddy was my oldest, most experienced dog. What was she thinking? Feeling furious and embarrassed, I didn't take Diddy to work with me for two full weeks. What it took me a stupidly long time to realise was that it wasn't Diddy's fault. It is *never* the dog's fault. When I stopped sulking and actually looked back at the situation from Diddy's perspective, she hit the right spot. She didn't cast (run in a wide arc) around to where I wanted her, but that's not where the movement of the mob was telling her she needed to be. I couldn't draw her a map with the plan laid out in detail, so she worked with what she knew. What she did was technically correct. I hadn't set the situation up right for her to understand what I wanted and that was on me.

It was an important lesson, one I needed to learn, and one I have not forgotten. It translates beyond dogs to all livestock and also to people. Take a second to try to see the situation from another perspective and maybe it will give you a whole new appreciation for why things happen the way they do. It might save you from overreacting to a situation, misplacing the blame and having to eat humble pie which, take it from me, is not a pleasant experience.

What I also learnt that day was you never know what good might come out of a seemingly bad situation. After all the angst of worrying about Dad being witness to the whole debacle and thinking we had justified his doubts, I was told later his only comment was, 'Well, she did well to get them back in again,' muttered in grudging approval.

*

It was obvious that my dogs and I really needed some extra training on our commands. They needed to learn how to listen and I needed to learn to get the instructions right. When Neil McDonald runs a school, he has on hand a calm, cooperative mob of either weaner calves, goats or sheep that are well educated to dogs. These animals, called a trainer mob, are tolerant of untidy handling by green participants and over-zealous work by young dogs because Neil has spent the time to 'get them right in the head' (mentally tough) through education prior to the school. That's the type of animal you need to have on hand when you want to train a young dog so that you can remain in control of the situation.

Deciding I needed some more control in my life, my dogs and I set out to make our own trainers. By this stage, we were coming to the end of our cattle work for the year so I had limited options as to what I could use for a trainer mob. Our cattle were out on the run and our holding paddocks empty. Well, mostly. There were six heifers that we hadn't been able to get into the yards when we cleared one of the paddocks. Probably not how I would recommend people start but, at that point, I had to work with what we had. Four of the six were culled for bad temperament but the other two weren't much better. By installing the same spear-trap system Grandad used (and we still employ at times) around their only source of drinking water, I managed to trap the heifers in our holding paddock yards. This was the first win of the day, but we still had to get them home, which required a five-kilometre walk along the laneway. And even though the laneway was fenced on either side, that could prove more of a suggestion to a determined Brahman than an obstruction, so I was on tenterhooks, waiting for at least one of them to jump. Those five kilometres turned into about eight as the heifers, dogs and I zig-zagged our way along the lane, arguing the whole way about which direction we should be going and whether they should stay together as one mob. The dogs and I won eventually and, as we retired for the night, I considered it a victory that at least our newly appointed trainers were home.

And so began the learning curve of creating a trainer mob. The biggest lesson I learnt from those heifers was the importance of reading your livestock's mental state. There was one heifer in this mob that would not settle and stay with the others. She seemed to prefer trying to climb out of the yards than complying with anything I was trying to do, and in the end I cut her out on her own and just continued working with the five others. That night, after spending an afternoon on her own in a separate yard, I put her back in with her mates. The next day, she didn't put a foot wrong. In hindsight, it's likely she was more sensitive to my insensitive handling than the other heifers, and the dogs and I kept over-pressuring her. Once she got hot in the head, she stopped thinking and just kept reacting, which was never going to end well for any of us. The best thing I could have done at that point was give her some time and space to cool down, as I did, but with better handling, she wouldn't have needed it to begin with.

*

Those heifers turned out to be an amazing trainer mob. The dogs and I spent many an hour with them, making up new challenges as we went, like bending (turning) around old yard posts and picking a gap between drums. I soon learnt that if I planned a path or destination that I could concentrate on instead of just wandering with no sense of direction, everything flowed better. My body language indicating where we were headed was clearer to both the dogs and the heifers, making it easier for them to follow my lead. When Dad asked why I needed to spend so much time working with my dogs, I replied, 'It's like when you buy a new bull wagon, Dad. You can't just take it straight out to a muster. You need to put a

Training trainers with Zen while my other dogs watch and wait.

bull bar on it, fit it out with the right tyres, weld some mesh over the windscreen and get a two-way radio working in it. Well, I'm just putting a bull bar on my dogs.'

Four of those six previously culled heifers in my original trainer mob became so well mannered they were retained as breeders. It goes to show that sometimes bad temperament is just a symptom of bad handling. It's on us to learn how we can do it better.

Chapter Seven

Pilbara Working Dogs

'If you think you have a good dog, you have a good dog.'
– Bud Williams, stockman

Murray and Del built a house on the southern farm near Dad's cottage and soon welcomed their first child, Odelia, into the world. Though Murray still managed the station through the busy mustering season, we knew it couldn't continue indefinitely. My days of being his right-hand woman who could spend half her time hiding behind a camera lens were on borrowed time.

My interest in photography had begun after a four-wheel-drive group passed through our property in 2011. One of the travellers in the group asked if she could come back sometime

The homeward stretch.

and photograph one of our musters. Helen had a lovely Scottish accent and I was fascinated by her ability to see something special in the seemingly ordinary. She captured the magic of the muster with her camera and now, ten years on, the photo-book she gave us is a precious keepsake of earlier days.

Running with the notion that the best camera is the one you have on you at the time, I started taking photos with my phone before eventually upgrading to a digital camera with a quality lens. Ironically, it is an early photo taken with my phone that has remained one of my most popular, a sepia image captured in the broken and dusty glass of my rearview mirror of our cattle droving along behind. You can see it on page seven of the picture section.

Upgrading to a real camera was a pivotal moment in my photography career. And a memorable one. The same day I bought it, after seeking advice from numerous photography friends and Google, I headed into a paddock at the farm to feed out hay to a mob of cows and calves. There was a gorgeous little calf of the darkest Brahman red, only a few days' old and fearless. With the cows distracted by the fresh hay, I hunkered down and snapped away, trying to focus in on his extraordinary, almost snake-like eyes.

One of the best pieces of advice I ever read when it comes to framing a shot was that when you see a scene that you think will make a good photo, stop and take a moment to recognise what it is that has captured your attention; then make that the focus of your photo. To whoever came up with that bit of advice, thank you. It's priceless.

It was while I was crouched low, thinking about this and crooning nonsensically to Mr Blue Eyes that I noticed a flicker of movement behind him. Taking one last shot, I peered up from behind the lens to see a rather unimpressed cow barrelling towards me, objecting to my interest in her baby. I sprang upright and leapt towards the ute, leaving her snorting behind me before she drifted back to the hay with her calf in tow. Deciding prevention was the best cure for bruises, I headed back for the house. In that last shutter click, I had got my shot. Captured perfectly in focus, with half his face and one big Brahman ear framing his beautiful eye, I fell in love with the image. And to this day, it is one of my personal favourites.

*

In 2014 I attended my second and third Neil McDonald schools, in quick succession. I hadn't realised how beneficial doing two schools back to back could actually be. After the first one, you stop worrying about making a fool of yourself, and things really start to click during the second. The first school was held back on the Geraldton property where I had first attended the year before; the second I helped organise to be run on a station a little north of us. It was while I was at Geraldton, though, that I had the opportunity to purchase Chrissie, a beautiful red-and-tan bitch who, unbeknown to me at the time the deal was struck, had a bellyful of puppies.

Chrissie was an exceptionally talented lead dog, who had a natural ability to read the movement and intentions of livestock. Natural lead dogs love working at the front of a mob, keeping the cattle walking steadily as they strategically give ground in front of them and essentially, as the name suggests, lead the mob. A joy to watch work, Chrissie was all style and speed with intense concentration, focus and often very little sense of self-preservation. She and her mini-me daughter, Jinx, are responsible for a lot of my grey hairs.

If there is a dog who lives up to the saying 'With the rose of brilliance, comes the thorn of temperament', it's Chrissie. She could be a bitch, in every sense of the word. Chrissie hated other dogs, especially females. She would tolerate Zen, my original castrated male, but no one else, and it didn't seem to matter what I did to try and make her more team-friendly, she remained stubbornly grumpy. It was hard to hold that against her, though, because it was the reason I was able to buy her, after her previous owner got fed up with her snarkiness. As much as she didn't like other dogs, she loved people. Her loyalty, love and companionship were second to none ... when she wasn't grumbling.

Chrissie blessed me with eight beautiful pups and throughout the course of raising, loving and watching those gorgeous bundles of talent find their feet in their new homes, my accidental journey into breeding working kelpies began. One in particular, Miss Jinx, made her mark in no uncertain terms on my recently established Pilbara Working Dogs Facebook page, at just three months old.

Miss Jinx and her seven red-and-tan siblings were born on 1 April 2014, so of course they all had to have April Fools names like Riddle, Hoax, Havoc and Houdini. Jinx didn't stand out from the other four girls in the litter at first, she was one of three very similar looking pups in between the runt and a large girl with pale features who I had my eye on. It wasn't until I was woken at a god-awful hour of the night to the terrified screams of a two-week-old pup with a large centipede attached to her foot that she suddenly became her own identity. From that day on, she wore a scar on her foot and I swear gained an extra dose of sheer grit and an unusually high pain threshold to go with it.

In the end, it felt like I didn't have a choice in which pup I retained. I used to look at the bigger girl and say, 'I really want to keep you,' then mutter as Jinx confidently crawled onto my lap like she owned me, 'but I feel like I have to keep you ...' So at eight weeks old, I started carrying her everywhere with me and her character and personality blossomed once she was away from her siblings, who headed off to their new homes a few weeks later. She rode front and centre on the motorbike like the queen she was, her head resting back against my chest.

As she grew bigger, creeping up past my chin as she perched in front of me on the bike, her red kelpie head finally filled my whole area of vision. If I dared complain about it, a wet tongue would periodically sweep back over her shoulder to shush me up. It was pretty effective.

When Jinx was three months old, we had some sheep turn up at the station, primarily to train my pups with but eventually they would fill the freezer to give us a change from beef. Due to the thorough spoiling Jinx had been receiving, there was some doubt around the camp as to whether she would deign to even look at the sheep, let alone be interested in working. But she quickly divested any non-believers of that notion. As soon as I set her down in the hay-laden yard, she was 'switched on' and working, to the surprise of all of us watching. She had the fast, low style of her mother, covering the skittish sheep with instinct like I'd never seen. Skidding to a halt in the hay and locking them in place with an intense stare, it was incredible to watch these skills in a pup so young. It was only after I had convinced her the job was done (okay, I had to nearly rugby tackle her to catch her in flight) that we noticed she had a swollen joint on her back foot. Apparently even at three months of age, a suspected broken toe wasn't going to stand in her way.

When she was four months old, I put Jinx back on the sheep, who were still no quiet trainer mob. Her natural talent, speed and agility at such a young age left me speechless. She was a rare gift that I was entirely unequipped for, considering how green to the dog world I was. Eight years on, I still feel green and unequipped but I'm getting better at bluffing my way through.

*

By the end of 2014, I knew it was time for me to take on the manager's role so Murray could see more of his family, but I wasn't yet ready to live life permanently on the station. Not yet. I was happily single, with my dogs unexpectedly granting me the confidence to stretch my wings, and I didn't want to be tied down like I was already married with kids. It was an amazing opportunity that was being offered to me – a chance to steer the station in my own direction, incorporating my dogs into every aspect I could – and I wasn't taking that lightly. I didn't want to walk away from it completely, I just needed the chance to travel, to try different work with my dogs, to attend dog schools, and to meet all the handlers I'd only heard about.

So an agreement was struck. I would take on the manager's role throughout the year and travel between our busy times. It didn't take me long to take advantage of this new-found freedom. In March 2015, my dogs and I hit the road.

Chapter Eight

Kelpies and Country Girls

'There's a difference between making a living and making a life.'
– Anonymous

The ochre-red river water swirled high around the truck's tyres as it gamely grappled for purchase against the strong pull of the current. The chain stretched taut against the bull bar and the grader lugged down for a beat, testing the weight behind before it started pulling.

'Well, that's one way to make it a memorable trip!' I thought, as I watched Neil McDonald's truck, dogs and all, get towed across our flowing Henry River. The joys of having an 88-kilometre dirt driveway with two river crossings. It always pays to have a backup plan.

Although the rain made things very touch and go for the dog school I was attempting to host on Glen Florrie in 2015, the first of many and a great success, the late-season fall was a wonderful blessing. We hadn't had any significant rain in the summer months leading up to this point and we had made the call that if it didn't rain in March, we would start our annual mustering lap early to take the pressure off the remaining feed. In the last few days of the month, we had enough rain to give the country a decent drink, allowing the mustering to be pushed back till June. It also allowed me to join one of my best friends and fellow dog enthusiast, Courtney, on a six-week road trip.

Courtney had grown up on her family station about 400 kilometres south of Glen Florrie in the Gascoyne. She had attended the same School of the Air as Murray and I had, though it wasn't until I got into working dogs that we met again and our friendship blossomed. She had become a capable and competent cattlewoman in her own right and we bonded quickly over our mutual love of dogs, photography and the country lifestyle. Courtney had started her journey into dogs when she purchased a well-bred bitch pup called Meg, who turned out to be a very talented kelpie. She slowly retained a few of Meg's progeny until she had a very handy team of dogs. Her kelpie stud name Killili is inspired by the name of the bridge near her home town. When I broached the idea of a joint road trip, leaving the station in the care of my family, Court was all for it.

Court and I hit the road – just two girls, one ute, a trailer, quad bike, nineteen dogs between us and no set plans – and it felt like we were flying free. A once-in-a-lifetime trip that I would do again in a heartbeat.

One of the first things Court and I noticed as we tried to skirt our way around the bustle of Perth was that our navigational skills off-farm were severely lacking. It seemed every turn we took was the wrong one and we hadn't even left our home state yet! This was a pattern that repeated itself time and again over the next six weeks, sending us sneaking around a mining camp near Norseman, Western Australia, late one night and driving north through Queensland for a good hour before we realised we were meant to be going south. That one's on me – Court was asleep in the passenger seat. The most memorable mistake, though, was near Lightning Ridge in New South Wales and recalling it makes me laugh to this day.

Courtney was peering at the mud map scrawled in a small notebook, given to us by a friend and containing somewhat vague directions on how to get to our next destination.

'Um, Court ... why does this fence look familiar?' I was getting a feeling of deja vu as I stared at the driveway we were currently cruising past.

Court glanced up then did a double take. 'Oh my god, go! *Go!* Quick, before they see us!'

We bolted, travelling along the same road we had driven only an hour earlier when we left the farm. We pulled up again at the gravel intersection at the end of the track. Reassessing the map, it was obvious we had missed a turn somewhere along the way, maybe more than one, but the fact that we had cluelessly driven in a full circle had us in stitches. Thank god for secondary fuel tanks.

*

While exploring Victoria, Courtney and I attended a Greg Prince dog-training clinic in Gippsland, along with Neil McDonald. It was a wonderful two days of learning from a legend of the dog world, well known as one of the most talented trainers and triallers around. Many of the lessons I learnt at Greg's clinic I still use today in my training. He had some effective techniques to even dogs up on their sides and keep them moving instead of letting them get too 'sticky', where they stayed too long in one place, as Jinx was prone to do. Just as people are usually more dexterous in either their left or right hand, dogs can also have a preferred side to work stock. These simple tricks have come in handy more than once with different dogs in my team.

My dogs were definitely bush dogs come to town, nestled in amongst predominantly collies, whose owners were mostly a few generations older than Court and me. It was amazing to see the control Greg and some of the other handlers had over their collies. I had a feeling that wasn't going to be where I ended up with my kelpies, though. This proved true when I headed out into the paddock with Diddy, ready for the next training exercise, which involved casting. This is when you ask a dog to run out wide and collect up a mob of animals. Some dogs have a naturally wide cast, some don't. Diddy was my best caster at the time, usually kicking out so wide my closer working dogs would have the job done by the time she got there. Not this day.

The rest of the participants had very well-controlled dogs who were taking Greg's lessons in their stride, many of them regulars. My dogs and I were quite a bit less graceful, but I thought with this task, at least, Diddy and I had a chance to prove we weren't complete beginners. My task was to send Diddy around a pen of sheep situated in the middle of the paddock and immediately adjust my position so I was close enough to the sheep to encourage her to stay out wide. Ideally, a dog should cast evenly around the mob, as wide around the side of the mob as they are deep when they come in behind them. The purpose of a wide cast is so the stock are left undisturbed by the dog until the dog is in position to control the stock. If the stock sight the dog too early and are particularly fresh or flighty, it can potentially be the difference between a successful gather and a blown mob, as it's known when they run away.

I cast Diddy out, fully expecting her to run wide or 'kick out' as she normally does, but instead, at first sight of the sheep, the novelty of handling these fun creatures took over her training and she made a beeline directly for them. She beat me to the sheep by a mile, before kicking out and around at the last minute, so her usual wide cast looked distinctly more lightbulb in shape.

Greg Prince chuckled at my embarrassment and offered reassurance. 'Don't worry about it. That's what we call a bushman's cast.'

Of all the days, Diddy ...

*

My original team of five dogs had grown over the last two years to a handy ten. Two of these were young males of similar age that I had purchased as pups. Strych, named as such after his parents, Cydie and Poison, was a fine-boned black-and-tan dog with striking pale tan features and intelligent eyes. Diego, the other half of the pair, was bred by Neil McDonald and was a strongly built strapping young dog with a lovely nature. Together, they were trouble.

'Strych! Diego!' My voice was hoarse from yelling as I ran towards the mob of circling cattle. 'Okay, this is not good,' I muttered as I caught glimpses of my errant dogs spurring the cattle on.

Courtney and I had joined Neil on another property in Gippsland to help him run a school for locals in the area. Our camp was set up near a line of trees with paddocks on either side, one of which held a mob of cattle. The same mob of cattle my two teenage dogs were currently using as an excuse to entirely ignore me. Leaving the camp of their own volition as they'd done is not a good habit for any dog, nor an easy one to break once it's established. It's even worse if you are at someone else's place and your dogs are chasing their stock, uninvited. I eventually got the two pups back but it was time to do something more about teaching them they couldn't disappear as soon as my back was turned.

That evening, after the school was done for the day, Neil waited near the mob of cattle with a stock whip in hand as I unloaded the pups and headed off for our usual walk along the laneway. It didn't take Strych and Diego long to see the cattle and take off towards them in search of some fun. This time, though, when they got near the stock, they were met with a loudly cracking whip. Realising they had been sprung, they soon hustled back to my side. It only took one more similar exercise before the lesson was learnt and the young dogs pulled their heads in.

High work drive is a very good thing and with these two dogs there was little risk of scaring them off wanting to get out there. But dogs need to have respect for the leader along with their drive, and, with Neil's help, we reasserted that. It was a very valuable lesson for me on the importance of pack manners.

*

It was at this school that I finally met the lovely Margareta Osborn in person, after we had chatted online about dogs for some time. Writer, wife, mother, and farmer of a beautiful property east of Melbourne, Margareta's plate was already full, but when she mentioned her son Callan's dream of owning a kelpie, I had suggested she get in touch with Neil McDonald about his upcoming school nearby. Well, in the same state at least. Unfortunately for Callan, he had a prang on his motorbike two weeks before the school was due to be held, but he didn't let a broken leg stop him from attending. Hobbling around on crutches, he did his best to learn what he could, though he later declared: 'I wouldn't suggest doing that again! It hurt too bloody much!!' Soon after, Callan acquired his first working dog, a young kelpie pup called Crosby.

Margareta generously invited us back to her farm, where we met the rest of her gorgeous family, husband Hugh, daughter Katie and older son Brent. After a few weeks on the road sleeping in our swags wherever we were parked, the comforts of a real home seemed almost luxurious. A roaring fire, a beautiful roast meal and easy, flowing conversation had us never wanting to leave. Our dogs enjoyed running over the

Neil McDonald, showing us how it's done. (Steve Strike / Ambience Entertainment)

lush green hills. Perhaps Margareta didn't expect there to be quite so many. She still recalls how they 'just kept coming!' as we let the dogs out of their cages that first afternoon. Only a few short months later, Margareta, Hugh, Katie, Callan and Crosby would pack up their car and head across country to join us for a season at Glen Florrie, cementing a friendship that still stands the test of time and distance.

*

After enjoying the cold April weather in Victoria, Court and I headed north into Queensland to attend a Faansie Basson dog school. Faansie is a well-known dog trialler, originally from South Africa, where he won many national sheep-dog trials before he and his family moved to the United States. I hadn't heard of Faansie before but Courtney was keen. So we incorporated it into our trip and arrived at the hosting farm the evening before the school was due to start. When I realised the calibre of the other attendees, experienced triallers with mostly collies, I had a sense of deja vu from the Greg Prince school, albeit this time with a younger crowd.

It was a very interesting few days. Faansie was open in talking about his experience in the military and how he applied that to his dog training. In some respects, Faansie's style didn't suit me or where I wanted to go with my dogs but, at the same time, some of the techniques he showed us have worked well over the years. It was a good opportunity to learn more about myself as a dog handler, while appreciating that I didn't have to take on everything a trainer taught. I could pick and choose what suited me and my dogs. I still maintain that it is worth getting to as many dog schools as you can, there is always something to learn. In some cases it may be simply realising what you don't want to do, though Faansie's school held more value than that for me.

After the school, Courtney and I took the opportunity to drive around the Queensland farm with Penny, the host. As well as her collie dogs, Penny also had some beautiful Italian maremma guardian dogs. These large dogs with fluffy white coats looked incongruous in the setting of an Australian farm, so far from their native land. This was the first time I had seen guardian dogs in action and the seed was planted that maybe there was a role for them in our system back home. Penny owned around fourteen maremmas, which stood guard over everything on the farm from goats and sheep to horses, cattle and the house itself. Our own dogs stayed locked up back in our ute at the house, because, as Penny explained, the maremmas were used to her collies but might consider the kelpies a threat. There are lots of stories demonstrating how you have to be careful not to over-handle maremmas or they won't do their job properly. Stories of these dogs being left out with the stock and having little or no human contact were not hard to come across, yet this was not what we experienced with

Penny's guardian dogs. As we headed out on her quad bike to where the sheep were grazing, Penny sent one of her collie dogs around the mob to bring the ewes across to us. Watching the maremmas glide through the sheep as if they were one of them was surreal. We stepped off the quad bikes and I pulled out my camera. Suddenly we were surrounded by large white dogs as they came from all parts of the farm to check us out. Thinking we wouldn't be able to get too close, I was crouched down with the long lens when a large white form floated past my viewfinder and nearly pushed me over. Turns out this particular male wasn't so shy after all.

Hearing Penny talk about how the dogs would band together to protect the stock from wild dogs was fascinating. On some occasions, she had lost young maremmas to wild-dog attacks but she maintained the maremmas were crucial in saving her stock from predation. After seeing this different approach to predator control, I was determined to work out a way to incorporate these amazing animals into our operation at home. It took me three years but I finally did get pups from Penny and it was one of the best decisions I've made.

*

Conveniently, our trip worked in with the famous Beef Week Expo in Rockhampton, which is held every three years. Featuring everything to do with cattle, from newly designed

Using a long-range lens to photograph a standoffish maremma ...

... or maybe not. (Bush Chooks Photography)

yard set-ups to exhibit livestock, cattle studs featuring their finest, and restaurants enjoying the end results, it's a week held in high regard by many in the industry.

Originally, Courtney and I had hoped to hold a joint stall onsite to sell our photography, but logistics and expenses soon disabused us of that notion. It was great to catch up with friends from back home, including my brother, who, without fail, always loses his voice on the first day due to his penchant for knowing everybody. While he still had some trace of his voice, he filled me in on the news of Glen Florrie. Everything was holding together and the late rain had produced the feed we hoped it would. Pressure was still off and the road trip could continue.

Seeing the cattle-dog trials in real life, actually the first trials I had ever seen, period, was a highlight for me. So was learning that my travel buddy had a very real fear of frogs – one I don't share. Driving back to our camp outside of town one night, Courtney nearly gave me a heart attack when she let out a shrill scream from the passenger seat beside me.

'Holy heck, what?! What is it?'

I peered through the dark windscreen, expecting to see an errant creature wandering across the road in the middle of the night. Preferably not a person.

'There's a frog!'

Courtney had crammed herself as far back into the corner of the cab as she could go, which wasn't far. I peered out again, a bit more short-sighted this time. Sitting outside the ute, perched precariously on the windscreen wiper, was the little amphibian in question.

'A frog? Are you kidding me? I thought I was about to hit something!' We couldn't help but laugh as the adrenalin rush slowly wore off.

'And yet you didn't even slow down,' Court mused.

Maybe I'd spent too many years driving bull wagons ...

*

It was while we were in Queensland that I picked up one of the best dogs I will ever have the pleasure of knowing. I had agreed to purchase Jasper a few months earlier from Cailyn, a mutual friend and fellow student of Neil McDonald. I had met Cailyn and her partner, Frank, when they spent a few weeks at the station one February, helping build a large cable cooler yard (a big yard for letting cattle cool down after mustering, which could also double as a weaner educating area) in the lovely heat of summer. She believed this dog had the makings of a great worker but he was excess to her needs at the time, so I took advantage of the opportunity to expand my numbers with some fresh blood.

The first time I met Jasper, it felt like I was reuniting with an old friend. He fitted into my camp like he'd always been there. He was a happy-go-lucky dog, his age unknown (somewhere between twelve and eighteen months was the best guess) and his experience minimal. I never really did any specific training with Jasper; he just learnt on the job. And yet he is the dog I have the best control over, the most pliable to commands. Jasper turned out to be a near perfect allrounder. He has a well-timed bark, will bite the front foot and nose of a recalcitrant beast, and rates his stock well, giving them relief naturally. He's my go-to dog if a job needs a bit of finesse and direction.

Of course, he's got his faults too. Jasper's biggest one is he loves calves. Obsessively, if I let him. And I don't mean in a good way. It's a frustrating habit when dogs develop a fascination with the smaller animals in the mob. Nothing worries a cow more than watching her calf being stalked and crept up on by a predator, and when a dog is fixated on one animal, they aren't concentrating on the job at hand. It's understandable in a lot of ways, because young stock are usually quicker to move, faster to react and more exciting to chase, but frustrating for me nonetheless.

Jasper was castrated just before I picked him up. I have mixed feelings about that decision, now that I have seen his talent, but the conformation in his back legs isn't great. He's bow legged – or cow hocked, as it's known in cattle terms – and that's not a good trait to breed on.

Being 'two stones lighter' didn't stop him from being a ladies' man, though, as I found out a few months down the track. One of my bitches, Bindi, had come in season and while I set up my dogs' gang chain (a long chain with short tethers spaced along it) under a big shady tree, I let all my dogs out bar Bindi. Once I had things sorted, I secured my two entire males and let Bindi out to stretch her legs. Obviously I wasn't supervising closely enough, because I turned around to find her knotted up with a dog. Quickly scanning the area in disbelief, I saw that my two males were still secure and partnerless. The culprit was Jasper, who very quickly got a thorough check over to make sure the vet hadn't missed something important during the castrating process. I didn't think it was possible, but Jasper seemed to have figured out a way to have the fun without the consequences. Life with these dogs is never boring, that's for sure. Especially with this goofy, talented clown.

*

Though we had originally intended to head home across the top of Australia, completing a full lap of the country, our plans changed somewhere along the way. We had made some good friends back in South Australia and were keen to catch up with them again before we headed home. We had both also long been fans of Scott and Trish Amon's Barru Working Kelpies Stud near Coffs Harbour in New South Wales, so we took the opportunity to visit on our way past to South Australia. Scott has carried on the old Karrawarra lines of the well-respected author and dog handler Tony Parsons, and it was wonderful to see these dogs in person.

What wasn't so wonderful was Scott's pet snake, Sammy, a small Woma python, which he proudly pulled out to show us. Snakes are not my favourite creatures in the world. I'm about as fond of them as Courtney is of frogs. Unfortunately, I have come to accept that snakes and I have to coexist on dry land so I took the proverbial bull by the horns and gingerly held Sammy aloft. At a distance. For about three seconds. It may not have been a prolonged experience but I still claim it as handling a snake, a small triumph over my fears and one I never plan to repeat.

While Court and I were visiting, one of Scott's bitches was due to whelp. Lucky for us, she decided the night of our visit was the time to start. Not so lucky for me, her whelping box was in the laundry, directly opposite the head of my bed on the other side of a very thin wall. We were both awake well into the night as she loudly voiced what I can only assume was her unflattering opinion of the male responsible.

After seeing the quality of Scott's dogs, Court decided to join her dog Meg, who had come in season while we were on the road, to Luke, one of Scott's sires. This was a decision I am extremely grateful for, as it produced the two talented Killili dogs I have in my team now, Diamond and Cash.

*

One of our last stops before we headed back across the Nullarbor towards home was a sheep station north of Port Augusta where a shearing school was being held. Peter Barr, a well-known dog trialler who we had met earlier in the trip and one of the friends we wanted to catch up with again, was working the sheds penning up the sheep for the shearers. Peter Barr was also the breeder of Chrissie and Jinx's line, so I was more than keen to see his dogs in action. We weren't disappointed. A mix of kelpies and collies, Peter's dogs were all well trained, barking on command, running along the sheep's backs and leaping over gates with an ease I could only envy. What makes Peter's skill with training dogs even more remarkable is his ability to use his voice, feet and eyes in lieu of his arms. Born with shorter arms and a few missing fingers like his father, and inheriting the same nickname of Twisty, Peter's skill with his team is impressive to watch.

At the end of the day, we headed out to where those of us with teams of dogs had them set up, five teams in all with who knows how many dogs between us. When we pulled out the feed bowls with dry food and lay down some fresh meat, it was amazing to watch all our dogs freely intermingle with no fights. Even a couple of big 'kangaroo dogs' joined in the feast. At one stage I had twelve dogs eating from the food bowl I had laid down but only six of them were mine. What made this possible was all five teams were used to being communally fed, with no bickering or fighting over food.

Outside of Court's dogs sharing feed bowls with mine, I had never seen communal feeding on such a scale – the manners instilled at home translating between multiple teams of dogs on the road. Dogs which, for the most part, had never met each other before that night and would likely never meet again. Try as I might, I just couldn't picture our heelers at home behaving quite so tolerantly.

Later that night, I heard the dogs fire up barking.

'Peter, how do you teach them not to do that?' I asked as we stood around the campfire, enjoying the warmth from the flames.

Peter shrugged. 'I don't. I like to let my hair down at the end of a day, so why can't they?'

I've always remembered those simple words, and when the dogs settled not long after, I thought maybe he had a point. They work hard all day, taking commands and living by the rules. Why not let them enjoy a little bit of freedom after the job is done?

Those last few days, capturing moments in the sheds and evenings around a campfire with good company and great music, were a fitting end to our incredible trip – although I knew it wouldn't be the last time my dogs and I trekked across the Nullarbor.

Chapter Nine

Life Lessons and Learning Curves

'Livestock recognise our movement and intentions well before we realise we are influencing them.'
– Neil McDonald

After returning home from my jaunt over east, mustering was soon in full swing. Margareta and her family arrived with just enough time to unpack before we all headed out to stock camp. We have a caravan set up with fridges, a (sometimes) hot shower and cupboards for all the paraphernalia that we require to survive away from the homestead for a week at a time while out mustering. Meals are cooked on the open fire (most are precooked at home in the slow-cooker and only require heating up), swags rolled out under trees and portable yards set up ready for the cattle to be mustered into.

We gave our weary Victorian visitors no time to settle in before we were off to a muster east of the homestead in country that we leased from the station next door. It must have taken the 'isolated in the middle of nowhere' vibe to a whole new level and left our new crew members wondering what they were in for. As it turned out, we were barrelling towards a tragedy.

Where we were mustering, our breeders had merged in with large numbers of feral cattle. It was a long few weeks, working from dawn to dusk, mustering, trucking, drafting cattle, shifting portable yards, fixing vehicle breakdowns, tyres and tempers. We were finally seeing the light at the end of the tunnel, with scrub bulls yarded up back at the homestead and ready to truck south to the abattoir.

These bulls are the kings of the bush, some weighing over 700 kilograms and fearing nothing but stronger bulls. Once captured, they were unimpressed and unfriendly, and took some careful manoeuvring from the top rail to the drafting yards. Usually we are more concerned about getting injured by a bull's horns or getting pinned against a fence by their bulk, but for my dogs it's a different danger they have to watch out for. These bulls are unbelievably fast and can strike out with their front hoofs, throwing the full force of their weight behind the hit. One of the kelpie's best attributes is speed, but if they don't have the space to utilise that speed, things can go very wrong, very quickly. Working dogs in small yards with fast cattle is a recipe for disaster, as I was about to find out.

On this fateful day, we were loading the bulls onto the truck, with Chrissie and Diddy's help. We had worked through half of the mob before things started to go awry. The remaining bulls we were trying to load had moved into the last pen before the race, and had pulled up short, not wanting to enter the single-file space. Chrissie loved nothing more than the chance to bite a nose, and taking advantage of a lowered head, darted in to put some pressure on one of the larger bulls. Bite delivered, she turned to bolt back under the rail to safety. I could only watch in horror as the bull took offence and struck out with his front foot, catching Chrissie across the chest with a downward blow. Her frenzied yelping froze my blood, as she crawled under the rail then raced around the big yard, blinded by the pain.

'No! Chrissie!'

I caught hold of her when she doubled back, pulling her close as my knees hit the ground. I ran my hands over her body and immediately felt the spongy swelling across her ribs.

'It's alright, girl. Shh, please Chrissie, please be okay.'

I crouched in the dirt over Chrissie's hot, dusty body. I cradled her close as she took her last breath, the light of consciousness fading from her eyes. I slipped her collar over her head, sobbing. I had lost her, gone in the space of a heartbeat with a crushed ribcage.

'I'm so sorry, Chrissie. I'm so sorry I let you go in there.'

We buried Chrissie up near my old dog kennels. She had her last ride on her favourite quad to where Dad and I dug her final resting place, tears streaming down both our faces.

Dad pulled me close. 'I'm so sorry, Kid. I know how much she meant to you.'

*

The awful day didn't end there. I was destined to learn one of the hardest lessons of all. There are some battles we just can't win and, if we try, someone we love can end up paying the ultimate price.

Only an hour after burying Chrissie, my old girl Diddy was a fraction of a second too slow to get out of the way of another deadly front hoof in a bigger yard, where I believed she would be safe. It caught her in the stomach and though I hoped she had escaped the worst of it, I started to have doubts later in the evening. She seemed outwardly fine, not interested in her dinner, but still drinking water and alert. Something was off, though. We were all exhausted and I was emotionally wrung out in the aftermath of losing Chrissie a few hours earlier. After a phone consult with Del, we decided to see how Diddy went overnight; I would tackle the five hours to our nearest vet first thing in the morning if she hadn't improved.

In the end, she took matters into her own hands. My last memory of Diddy is seeing her standing calmly, watching me blearily head back to bed after checking on her again as I did each hour.

I paused to look back at her, noting that even in illness, she never lost her regal composure. 'Goodnight, old girl, I'll see you shortly.'

When I stumbled back out to check on her again, Diddy was nowhere to be found. I realised then that in those last few moments, she had said her final goodbye. We spent two days scouring the station, looking for any sign of her, with no luck. Margareta, Hugh, Callan and Katie spent hours walking up and down the river behind the house, searching for her tracks. We had just the week before agreed that Diddy deserved a lovely retirement on a farm in the Gippsland hills and would join Margareta and her family when they headed home. I guess it just wasn't meant to be.

In some ways, I am glad that she was able to choose her final resting place and go in peace. But I will always wish that she had let me be with her at the end. To thank her for everything, to say sorry once more for not being able to protect her and provide a little solace in those final moments.

*

While on the road with Courtney, I had managed to secure more than just the Osborn family to join our crew. Lachlan, from a sheep property in South Australia, had recently attended one of Neil's schools and was keen to work at a place where he could utilise his dogs in a similar manner. I was excited to have someone else with dogs on the station. Although we didn't really have enough work for two teams of dogs most days, the chance to share ideas and techniques was worth the extra downtime for my dogs.

A few days after Lachie arrived, I had a mob of 500 or so freshly weaned young stock in the yards. They just needed a bit of education before they would be marked and taken out to their new paddock. Up until then they had been mustered, handled through the portable yards, taken off mum, loaded onto a truck and left to rest in the homestead yards. After a few laps around the large yard which had been built with railway iron and cable for just this purpose, I decided we needed more room and should take the cattle out into the bigger but decidedly less secure cooler paddock. Up to this point, they had been extremely well behaved and had lulled me into thinking this was going to continue. I walked over to the double gates, swung them wide and headed out ahead of the weaners into the paddock, with Lachie alongside and our dogs jointly scattered around the place. So far so good.

Suddenly we had a rush of weaners tear past us, paying no mind to the dogs in front of them working in vain to steady the lead. As we stood there, watching the mob disappear out into Oozo's paddock (named as such after one of our original Brahman bulls), I regretted not shutting the next gate they were currently racing through. I could see panic starting to creep into Lachie's eyes. All our combined dogs were now working up front of the mob to get a block on the galloping weaners but they didn't appear to be slowing. To be honest, at this point, I wasn't feeling very cocky myself.

'Should we go get them? What do we do?' Lachie asked. This was a fair question. We currently had no cattle, no dogs and no idea of what was happening over yonder behind the trees.

'It'll be alright, they'll bring them back,' I said, trying to feign confidence. 'Maybe we'll walk down a bit closer, though, just in case they need a hand,' I hedged.

We reached the back of the cooler paddock with not a weaner to be seen but we could hear the dogs working further out in the river by the sporadic barks of Jasper and one of Lachie's dogs. Still maintaining a calmness that was actually slipping further with each passing second, I waited by the cooler paddock gate while Lachie jogged a bit further out into Oozo's paddock. Soon enough, the weaners started trickling back in, moving steadily in a mob back towards the yards with the panting dogs tucking the stragglers in on the tail. I shut the cooler paddock gate behind them (better late than never) and it wasn't until they were safely yarded up behind the double gates of the original cable yard that I finally released the breath I didn't realise I had been holding.

'I've never seen anyone stay so calm in a situation like that! I thought we had lost them!' Lachie exclaimed once everyone was back to where they should be.

'Hands off the handlebars, Lach! I knew the dogs had them under control the whole time ...' I quipped, surreptitiously rubbing my sweating palms down my jeans.

*

There is a saying I heard at a timely point in my life: 'If a situation isn't going to be an issue in five minutes, tomorrow or even a week's time, it's not worth making a big deal over now.' It would have been less than ideal if I had lost the weaners into the paddock that day with Lachie but, at the end of the day, it was a paddock. It was fully fenced and there was only so far they could go. After they went through the process of being marked, that's where they were headed anyway. It might have cost us a day regathering them, but it wouldn't have been the end of the world. If that same situation had happened before I learnt the value of keeping my cool, I could have made things much worse.

The day I learnt this valuable lesson is not one I'm proud of. We have a long pen in our homestead cattle yards divided in two, and creatively called the top long yard and the bottom long yard. This day I was in the top long yard with four steers, letting them out a gate which was in a corner. The first three left with no issue, the fourth did not. He would run to every corner but the one with the open gate and it seemed no matter what I did he refused to see it.

In a fit of frustration I kicked out at the steer's rump as he circled me once more, looking for an escape. Of course, I was wearing my trusty double pluggers which were my preferred mode of footwear even in the yards. One step up from the barefoot kid I had grown up as, at least. I'm not the most coordinated soul at the best of times, so, of course, I mistimed my kick, and with only rubber thongs for protection, darn near dislocated my big toe.

Ironically, while I was cursing and carrying on, I inadvertently took the pressure off the steer who finally found the open gate and disappeared in a cloud of dust. As I stood there, nursing my tender foot, I realised that my hissy fit had achieved nothing except to make things more difficult for myself. Hindsight has also helped me appreciate that it was my poor stockmanship that made it difficult for the steer to understand where I wanted him to go in the first place. I was badly timing the pressure and offering no relief when he needed it, sending mixed messages with my body language. No wonder the poor thing was confused; he was too frazzled to think.

It's easy to get caught up in a situation and let our emotions rule our temper or, worse, our mouths and our actions, leading us to say or do something we later regret. So often it's over something that is forgotten in a few hours. Letting go of my quick temper has made life so much more enjoyable. Doesn't mean I don't still have my bad days where I lose my cool quicker than I should. But I am better at recognising those situations now and some days I'll even put my dogs away so they don't have to deal with me either.

*

Two months after our visit to Scott and Trish Amon, Courtney's Meg gave birth to the five pups she had conceived. Court had given me a choice between the two sisters in the litter, and there was something about Diamond's pale markings and 'I can take on the world all on my own' attitude that drew me in.

I remember the first time my no-affection-needed pup actually ran up to me for a cuddle – or so I believed. 'Diamond, what's going on? You never want pats!'

Suspicion soon turned to amused exasperation when I realised I wasn't looking at Diamond at all, but at Charm. Lachlan had done a sneaky collar swap between my two young females and Diamond was currently off gallivanting around, pretending I didn't exist, as per normal.

'Yeah, yeah, nice one, Lachie.'

That independent little pup has turned out to be one of the mainstays of my team and one of my best breeding bitches too.

With a wide cast, a no-nonsense nose bite and a long-legged body built for speed, she's a force to be reckoned with. She has an extremely strong heading instinct and also a very large presence on stock, all of which combined can drive me insane when we are working softer cattle. Handy if I am working harder cattle that need a bit more encouragement to pull up; not so handy when I'm trying to take a mob of breeders from A to B.

Diamond can also get herself into quite a tizz in some situations. She loves working the race but gets overexcited and bounces around on the spot whining while I'm trying to direct her anywhere but in front of me. But she's a machine in the yards. One video I posted on social media of my dogs moving a stubborn animal through the yards into the race was hugely popular thanks to Diamond. She was very carefully applying pressure to the animal to turn it around, and when it did and I asked her to 'stop', she froze immediately, paw still lifted in the air awaiting her next step. There's every chance she had planned to pause there anyway and I fluked the timing of the command, but it sure looks like I had her well trained for a minute there.

*

Two years into my journey with my dogs and I was starting to feel like we were finally getting the hang of things. I had come to appreciate one of the most important skills I require in my dogs: the ability and desire to work stock with minimal direction from me. This is where the kelpie's independent, headstrong nature really comes into its own. And as I have previously learnt, sometimes the best way to get a desired result with cattle is for me not to be involved.

One winter morning, I had headed out to our holding paddocks with my team of nine dogs, determined to have a win with a mob of cull cows. This wasn't our first attempt. Earlier in the week, we had tried to yard up the full mob of 350-odd cows, and to the dogs' credit they'd given it a good go. But the cattle had run back over them, heading at a quick pace to the relative freedom of the wide paddock.

I thought I'd be clever and block them up with the drone I was flying. To my surprise it worked! At least, it did for about four seconds. Then my signal failed and the drone's inbuilt safety mechanism had it flying directly back to where it had taken off from, happily ignorant of my panicked attempts to change its course. Nothing quite like a scary low-flying UFO buzzing over their heads to really give cattle something to be spooked by. Lesson learnt: sometimes you have to break a job down to bite-sized pieces.

What I also learnt from our previous attempt was how sensitive these cows were to my presence. With just the dogs out there, they were significantly more pliable, keeping their focus down low and on the dogs. But as soon as I was in the picture, all bets were off. They would hold their heads high, realising I was the real threat, and run over the top of the dogs who were valiantly trying to stay in front of them.

Over the ensuing days, we'd grabbed the majority of the cows out of the paddock, so my dogs and I were now charged with capturing the remaining 60-odd head, which had stubbornly refused our herding. Learning from the previous days, I cast the dogs out wide around the cows in the paddock as soon as we arrived and kept out of sight behind the ute, watching proceedings via my drone. As long as I stayed out of sight, I could offer encouraging whistles to let them know they were doing well, but the rest was up to them. Over the next half an hour, the dogs worked tirelessly to put the cows in the yards, with basically no help from me.

And they excelled. Even though it took two attempts and quite a bit of legwork, eventually the cows chose the path of least resistance. They walked in and stayed put in the yards until I could waltz over and chain the gates like I'd been out there helping all along. The dogs enjoyed a well-earned drink and swim in the trough while I truly counted my blessings at having these capable offsiders in my life. Nothing like a hard-earned win to really make you appreciate the miles it's taken to get there. Lucky for me the dogs haven't learnt to open gates or drive yet; then I would be nearly dispensable.

Watching the drone footage later that night, it was amazing seeing the dogs work from above; I could pick up how the cattle were influenced by their smallest movements, and vice versa. I also realised that the first yard-up wasn't successful because of one cow, just one, pushing her way back through the mob and stopping the flow into the yards. Something I couldn't see from the ground. Talk about annoying. But back to dogs.

I have always had a range of work styles in my team. Some of my dogs, like Jasper, have plenty of 'walk-up strength' and the confidence and presence to move in close to stock, biting a nose, over an eyebrow or front foot. These three areas are effective and considered 'fair' for a dog to bite if they need to put pressure on an animal. A dirty bite would be if a dog grabbed an ear, anywhere on the neck or shoulder, or, for me, the back leg. Heel bite is a dividing work trait amongst handlers in the dog world, much like bark seems to be. You either love it or hate it. As with bark, I believe it can be effective, if it is used at the right time in the right situation. However, personally, it reminds me of walking along the shopping aisle and copping a trolley to the back of the foot … it's infuriating.

Not all of my dogs have bite. Some rely on bark to work the cattle, though bark is really just a bluff if they don't have the bite to back it up. That's fine for soft cattle who move with minimal pressure, but for cattle who are less respectful, sometimes bark alone won't be enough.

I also have dogs that neither bark nor bite. These are generally my wider working, softer covering dogs. Invaluable

A rare photo of our family all saddled up ready to walk a mob of cows out to their paddock. Mum on Bandit, Me riding Taffy, Murray with old Marley, and Dad on his gelding, Cochise.

Decked out in my SOTA school uniform, complete with my missing front teeth, standing outside our cattle yards and pig pens.

Murray and Adele's wedding.

The ever regal Flora.

Miss Jinx.

Leah, my blue heeler, playing nursemaid
to an orphaned poddy calf.

Jasper, weary at the end of a long day mustering.

Cash Dog.

Murray and Bindi heading out in the station truck to pick up freshly mustered cattle.

Cruise, taking his first shaky steps after his near-death experience.

Sass is never one to pass up an opportunity for a cuddle.

When the cab of the truck just doesn't cut it.

Tailing the cattle in during a muster.

Sass teaching a mickey bull some manners.

Bindi and Tulli not at all daunted by the size difference.

Jasper teaching a steer some manners during our road trip in South Australia.

Chrissie with her pups, taking motherhood in her stride.

Unfortunate timing, sorry Sass!

Ang and Julia dancing through the prickles trying to bend a stubborn cow.

Dog tired. Sinner, Charm, Flora and Cruise taking the chance to nap on the back of the quad while Jasper steals the front.

Ang and Julia keeping an eye on our progress from the stock crates.

Holding the line.

Ringer keeping close to his mob of calves.

Bottle-feeding poddy calves.

Ringer's bath interrupted by a curious weaner.

Bringing cattle into our holding paddock yards.

By the time the twelve months of filming for the *Muster Dogs* documentary was wrapped up, Gossip and I had posing for the camera down pat. (credit Steve Strike / Ambience Entertainment)

The ever-handsome Cruise.

Gossip Girl at work.

Beautiful Blue Eyes, the turning point in my photography.

Me and my fellow *Muster Dogs* participants: CJ and Spice, Joni and Chet, Rob and Lucifer, Frank and Annie, me and Gossip. (credit Steve Strike / Ambience Entertainment)

Misty sheltering from the glorious drought-breaking rain as the rest of the team frolicked.

The promise of life with the flush of new germination.

The Wannery Creek as it curves behind our homestead.

Wildflowers in full bloom
as we finally reach the other
side of the drought.

Kelpies and cattle,
my favourite combination.

on softer stock, they can sometimes seem to have little influence on a bolder mob of cattle. But watching my dogs that day from the new overhead drone perspective showed me there was more going on than I could see from the ground.

Neil McDonald sums it up beautifully when he explains, 'The close dogs are working the bodies of the beasts, while the wider covering dogs are working their minds.' My stronger dogs were working within the cattle's flight zone, close in and putting pressure on the animals that were pushing against them. My softer-style dogs, who are very sensitive to the whole mob's flight zone, placed themselves out wider to cover the bigger picture. From the cows' perspective, those close dogs are the main pressure, but potentially escapable. When they look up and see a second line of dogs waiting further back, escape doesn't seem quite so easy. Nothing like a change in perspective to start seeing things in a new light.

*

My team had seen a few changes since the early days. Dogs came and went as I slowly got a feel for the type of dog that I needed and the type of dog I worked well with. Charm had joined the team as a seven-month-old pup from Peter Barr. I had asked him to keep an eye out for a bitch pup he thought might suit me after I lost Chrissie and Diddy, and he delivered exactly that.

Charm is a beautiful little dog with a very quirky personality and a lovely soft work style. She is a wider covering worker with no bark or bite but will cover any part of the mob and go all day. Often I will leave her out floating around the mob while droving, and it doesn't always go to plan. Charm will start working the side of the mob with me, then kick out to the lead to tuck in a few wandering stock before drifting around the other side of the mob (known as the wing) then creeping around to the tail.

It's sometimes at this point that confusion strikes and Charm suddenly decides I'm not where she left me (I am) and turns around from the back of the mob, running flat out retracing the way we have come. With surprising speed and agility, considering the shortness of her legs, she dodges all efforts at capture by anyone except me. The first time she did this, the helicopter pilot helping with the muster spotted the little black speck running full pelt down the track to the water point we had just left. He even tried to get her to slow down by hovering in front of her, with no luck. Once she's made the decision to float, there's no stopping her. As she has gotten older, she has become a little better at being picked up by others who manage to intercept her early, but if I ever need a tracking collar on a dog, it'll be this one.

Charm is loyal to the core, very much a one-man or, in this case, one-woman dog. She is sweet and affectionate to me and will tolerate affection from others if she must, though she is mellowing with age. There is only one thing Charm loves more than me. Food. She will skip out on walks and sneak up to the shed to chew a hole in a bag of dog food if I'm not watching. When I am away for a few days and Mum is looking after her, Charm will buddy up to Mum knowing she might get a meal. As soon as I return, though, she'll hide behind my legs like a child peeking around her mother's skirt and pretend she's never seen Mum before in her life. There is something about that beautiful loyalty that warms the heart of the lucky person who has earnt it.

*

Before I had my kelpies, I couldn't comprehend moving an older dog on to a new home. I believed that once you had a dog, it was with you for life and it wouldn't adjust well to the change. This could very well be true with pet dogs. Leah was one of these dogs. Even though I didn't need her in a work sense (she still loved to join in any chance she could, with mixed results), she would live out her days on the station with me. But for the most part, a working dog's first love is work, and if they go to another home where they are still able to work they will adapt well.

I was coming to realise that I don't suit every dog that I meet and not every dog that passes through my team will suit me. Just as every person we meet isn't someone we can be close friends with, the same applies to dogs. I have had the privilege of owning some extremely talented working dogs with brilliant breeding but which I have sold. For me, if we don't have the right bond, neither of us will see our full potential. Likewise, some of my best dogs have been moved on from other teams for not making the cut there. A dog might just need the right situation and handler for their personality before they can properly develop their talents. Flora, from my original four, was one of these dogs.

Flora was a beautiful black-and-tan girl with pale markings, floppy ears, beautiful brown eyes and a maturity beyond her years. Though she wasn't as pretty to watch work as Diddy had been with her full kit of commands, or as quick with her movements as Ang or Julia, Flora was soon showing me she was one of my better dogs.

Flora was a huge learning curve for me. When I started running a team of dogs, I thought I had to be tough with them or I would lose control of the situation. I couldn't stand perceived disobedience, especially as I was trying to convince myself I was capable of walking this new path I had set for myself.

Flora's independent, stubborn nature rubbing up against my own short-tempered ignorance led to quite a few run-ins. Flora also had a sensitive, standoffish personality, and was very slow to trust – the type of dog who could 'slip through the cracks', as Neil put it, if she ended up in the wrong hands.

But I was determined to be the right hands, and about three months into our journey and after a lot of persistent affection on my part, I finally won her over.

That was a turning point for us both. Flora learnt to trust and soon was free and easy with affection towards anyone she thought was a soft touch. Even those that weren't.

'Flora needs a collar that says "Free Pats", like one of those "Free Hugs" T-shirts,' Murray commented one day as we watched the dog in question sidle up alongside an unsuspecting victim. She would stare at them expectantly until a hand started rubbing her ears, like a subconscious gesture obeying a silent command.

'Yeah, yeah. I did all the work and now she just loves everyone,' I grumbled, but it was a lovely sight to see her so comfortable with people.

Although it drove me nuts most days, I soon realised that Flora's independence was her strength and she blossomed when I finally stepped out of her way. Over the years, she became the core of my team, the one I could use in all situations on every job. She had a good balance of eye, cover, stamina and bark. She would tail cattle all day on a muster, always shadowing the last beast in the mob, never leaving one behind. She would occasionally hitch a ride when it suited her. I could beg all I liked for her to come and get a drink but she agreed only when she was good and ready, lasting on the job longer than the rest of my dogs by far.

Flora didn't care who she worked for as long as they didn't try and tell her how to do her job. This included me. She would help walk weaners down the laneway to their new paddock, invaluable help for whoever was charged with that task as she flushed dawdling cattle out of the trees or steadied the lead if they started moving too fast.

Flora ended up being the only one of my original five dogs that stayed with me long-term. Julia was sold to a sheep farmer near Geraldton while I was attending a school there. Ang took Diddy's place with Margareta's family when they headed home to Gippsland, and Zen, my first pup, would soon find his new home on a property in South Australia, when I hit the road again.

Chapter Ten

Miles and Memories

'You will not do things differently until you see things differently.'
— Anonymous

I had never realised travel blues were a thing until Courtney and I returned from our road trip. It hit us hard. I'd had a taste of life on the road with my dogs and the pull to go back was undeniable. The station was ticking along well after experiencing a run of average wet seasons. Dad was prepared to spend the summer looking after things there while Murray and Del looked after the farm. Mum was spending the summer closer to her new granddaughter (and away from the Pilbara heat) so I took the opportunity to disappear back across the Nullarbor after a family Christmas at Grandma's.

Just before Christmas of 1981, Mum lost her father, Frank, to a heart attack. He left behind four daughters, Grandma, a bird park and a tree farm a little east of Esperance. Grandma continued to plant trees, show tourists through the bird park and old bottle collection while raising her youngest daughters. Throughout my childhood we spent most Christmases at Grandma's and I have so many wonderful memories of times there. Murray and I shared a room and would wake up in the morning to our stockings laid out on the ends of our beds. We were allowed to open these gifts from Father Christmas while we waited for the adults to wake up (carefully counting them to be sure we had the same number). At 6 am, we could race into Grandma's room to show off our bounty and marvel at Father Christmas's visit. In the lounge room, we'd find an empty cup and a few crumbs remaining from the milk and biscuits we had left out for him, and, outside, the remains of carrot his reindeers had devoured and a water bucket upended. I remember hearing a commotion one year outside our bedroom window and raced to the door to find Dad hopping around nursing a sore foot after tripping over said bucket. I was so disappointed it wasn't Father Christmas I didn't give much thought as to why Dad was actually out there.

While the adults got breakfast, we kids were tasked with carefully sorting the presents that lay under the brightly decorated Christmas tree into piles next to everyone's chairs in the lounge room. Murray and I would have already sifted through them so many times in the days leading up, that we pretty well knew ours by sight, but we'd always find a few hidden extras tucked in amongst the pine needles. The tradition on Grandma's side of the family is for one person to open a present at a time so everyone can appreciate the gift, and to very carefully unwrap the paper so it can be reused. Depending on how many other family members joined us, this could mean we were still opening presents when lunchtime arrived. I still love the practice, possibly more than some in-laws who have come to it later in life and are a little more used to the 'rip, tear and bust' method.

After lunch, the adults would head off for a sleep and Murray and I and any other cousins who were with us would bunker down in the lounge room to watch Christmas cartoons on video. Even now we do the same, though we have the next generation cuddled alongside to share them with.

Christmas traditions duly upheld, in late 2015 I packed up my ute and headed east again. This time I was on my own with only twelve dogs for company and three months of freedom to see where life took us. Eli, who had worked with us through the season, had built me a specially designed dog box for the back of my ute. Featuring four large cages underneath a storage compartment that provided insulation above, the dogs were set up and comfortable for the long trip. New Year's Eve was spent camped under the stars on a back road somewhere in South Australia, as I wondered what adventures the new year would bring.

*

The smell of burning feathers drifted past my nose as I struggled to keep my footing. One long leg struck out, catching me – more by accident than design – in the thigh with a sharp nail.

'Hey, come on, you ran into me!' I griped as I staggered back, watching the emu untangle himself from under my bike, losing a few more tail feathers to the hot exhaust pipe in the process. Soon enough he was free and took off across the paddock, dodging the saltbush scrub. I picked the bike back up, dusted off the seat and called Jinx over from where she waited nearby, as unimpressed as I was at the unexpected dismount.

Lachie, who had worked with us through the year, had lined up some goat mustering that I could help with on a property out near Broken Hill in western New South Wales. He had generously loaned me his near new 250cc motorbike for the week and now, two days into the job, I'd already laid it on the ground. Twice. In my defence, this last time wasn't intentional. I'd been racing along a fence line and come across an emu doing much the same thing on the other side, sans the bike. With limited experience of mustering emus, I expected him to move away as I continued along. Not so. He waited until I was level with him then vaulted over the fence and straight into the side of my front tyre. Jinx kamikazied over the handlebars as I let the bike drop and tried to jump back from the emu's thrashing legs.

'Well, that was fun,' I muttered as Jinx and I righted ourselves and headed on down the track. The smell of burning feathers followed us for the rest of the day.

It wasn't to be my last stack either. Later that day, as we tried unsuccessfully to stop a steady stream of goats from running past us – like water through a sieve is an accurate analogy – my bike and I disagreed on which way to go around a bush and I upended over the offending shrub. I hit the ground with a thud and lay there, trying to catch my breath while I catalogued new aches and bruises and mentally thanked Lachie for the foresight of a helmet. This goat mustering was a whole new ball game.

Goats, I learnt over the course of the week, were interesting creatures. When they got tired and sulky, nothing the dogs nor I could do would change their minds about staying planted under that tree. I'd finally met creatures more stubborn than me. They would lull you into a false sense of complacency – four mobs of five all moving towards each other nicely, letting you think this was a walk in the park. Then you'd crest a hill and suddenly notice all you had left was one mob of four. Once goats got it into their heads that they wanted to go in another direction, you'd have more luck holding back the ocean. And never let them near your bike's front wheel. If they swipe that out from under you, things are going to hurt. Take my word for it.

I learnt that goats respond exceptionally well to good stockmanship. If I handled them from a distance, giving them plenty of space, they became pliant and cooperative relatively quickly. In this way, they reminded me of feral cattle. I also learnt that five days straight on a narrow two-wheeler motorbike seat is more than I ever want to do. I would never complain about a quad bike again.

Jinx was my best goat dog. At one point, walking a fresh mob along, one old nanny kept spearing out the front, trying to lead the rest of the mob astray. Jinx would bite her on the nose anytime she ended up too far out front, turning her back towards the mob until she called a truce and led her band of followers at a steady walk. Jinx was also my smallest dog and the easiest one to chauffeur on the bike.

Jasper, my big goofball, loved riding on the bike with me. A lot more than I liked riding with him. He would launch off the bike as soon as I stopped and if I didn't get my feet quickly planted on the ground I'd find myself flying off the other side. Good times.

*

After my week with the goats, I headed further south. Neil McDonald had arranged a job for me with a friend and fellow dog man on a sheep property on the South Australian–Victorian border near Frances. This was a great opportunity for the dogs and me to sharpen up our stock skills, and sheep were an entirely new type of animal for us to work with.

On my first day, I was tasked with shifting a mob from the yards, down the laneway and into their new paddock. Pretty straightforward really. With map in hand, I headed out with Jinx, Jasper and the AG200 bike, same as I'd often ridden as a kid. After the sheep scattered into three mobs and I had ridden into the fence at least twice, I pulled up, regrouped and hoped to hell no one had been watching. This might be harder than I thought.

Once I settled in, I loved the work on the farm, shifting mobs between paddocks and bringing them into the yards ready for shearing.

Jasper, Charm and Jinx were my go-to dogs. Jasper, in particular, absolutely loved the sheep yards. He took to backing like, well ... a kelpie to sheep work, I guess. Though it took us a few hours longer than someone with a bit more experience, those afternoons I could spend working with my dogs as we filled the shearing pens in the shed with sheep were some of my favourites.

One of the biggest takeaways from this time as a contractor and farmhand was the experience of working for someone else. It gave me a chance to understand situations better from an employee's perspective, instead of an employer's. I noted the little things, like having a map of the property available, which I could use for easy reference, and being given a list of jobs then left to my own devices to get things done, that made me enjoy the work more. These were things I could implement back at home that would make me a better boss to work for.

*

While I was travelling around South Australia, my cousin Kristy, my aunty Marina and Grandma flew over for a week's holiday outside of Adelaide. I had conspired with my cousin to surprise Grandma and join them, but it nearly cost me a precious dog. Paul, who I had met during my trip with Courtney the year before, offered to look after my team alongside his while I played tourist in Adelaide. Paul was a shearing instructor when he wasn't a shearer himself and he often traded dogs as he travelled around shearing sheds and farms for work. A few days earlier we had agreed to swap my dog Diego for a pup of Paul's that had caught my eye. Paul was happy because he had someone he thought might be keen on Diego and could let the potential new owner see Diego over the weekend that I was away.

The next day, my phone buzzed with an incoming message. I read it as my cousin chauffeured us towards our lunch destination at Maggie Beer's Farmshop.

Got that bloke here looking at Diego and he really likes him! He asked if Diego could back and bark and when I asked Diego to speak up and jump on the sheep's back, he did! I think I can get a lot more than you thought for him!

Backing is when a dog jumps up and runs along the back of sheep, usually packed in a pen or race, with the purpose of either getting them to pack tighter for treatment like drenching or to keep them flowing, say, onto a truck. It's a very sought-after skill in dogs working sheep, as is bark on command. Huh, I thought, I didn't know Diego could do that. It was also not something many of my dogs could do. Apart from one, and he wasn't Diego.

'Wow, well, that's great. You've done well considering you've only officially owned him for a week.'

The excited reply came back quickly.

'I'll let you know how I go!'

A few minutes later I received a phone call.

'Are you sure this dog hasn't been castrated? I've had my hands near up to his throat and I still can't find anything!' Paul's exaggeration made me laugh out loud.

'Yes, of course I'm sure. They aren't exactly hard to spot!'

A photo came through on my phone of a dog's underside, splayed out enjoying a belly rub. I squinted at the familiar sight and alarm bells sounded in the back of my mind.

'Ah Paul? What colour collar has he got on?'

'An orange one ... '

'PAUL! That's Jasper, not Diego!! Of course, he backs and barks, he's my best dog! DO NOT SELL HIM!'

I can just imagine the conversation that followed, as Paul had to sheepishly admit that he had the wrong dog. Sadly, Jasper had set the bar too high and Diego didn't get sold that day. When I returned after the weekend, we decided to undo our deal and Diego continued with me for a while longer.

Though my cousin and I were lost in fits of laughter at Paul's blunder, it still gives me chills to think how close I came to losing Jasper, truly one of the most amazing dogs I will ever have the honour of knowing.

*

If it wasn't for one of my best friends getting married at the end of March, I'm not sure I would have headed home after my three months of freedom were up. That time on the road had helped me grow as a person and a dog handler. It wasn't until I was two days out from hitting the road home that I finally accepted the trip was over and I started looking forward to seeing the station again. We had received some decent rain late in January but no follow-up so we would be hoping for some winter falls to keep the country fresh.

I had missed my family while I was away but, in all honesty, I hadn't missed the business or the work that awaited me. I'd been able to switch off and live life as if the only responsibilities I had were my dogs. I relished that freedom and was lucky enough to experience it again in the years that followed.

In 2017, I realised a childhood dream of seeing Montana and Wyoming when I spent six weeks travelling through the United States with two great friends. And in late 2018, I returned on my own, visiting sledding dogs in Alaska, seeing the rodeo finals in Las Vegas and returning to Wyoming and Montana for a white Christmas with friends. Though I missed my dogs terribly, these opportunities to see the outside world were incredible and I thank my family for holding things together at home without me – and for looking after my dogs. The experience, knowledge and confidence I gained while away from home are making me a better manager now.

Chapter Eleven

Pups and Pedigrees

**'Breed of dog doesn't matter so long as it's one you like.
If you like the dog, you'll spend time with it.'**
– Greg Prince

I blew out a deep breath and watched the dusty cobweb dance barely two inches from my nose. I couldn't see the resident spider, which meant it had either scampered away or was already in my hair. At this point, I didn't particularly mind which, as long as it didn't consider me a meal and start biting. My bigger concern was snakes. I had a bad feeling the cool, dark, sheltered area under the old schoolroom that I was currently wriggling my way through would be their version of heaven. It seemed like my pregnant bitch thought it wasn't too bad either. Never one to do as she's told, Flora had decided the area I'd chosen for her to whelp in wasn't up to scratch and had sneakily carried one of her pups at two days old back under the old rooms to her original choice of nest. If it wasn't for the high possibility of snakes and the complete lack of human access, it would be perfect. But Flora's pups weren't going to get away with no human interaction for their first weeks of life, hiding under the building like recluses. And they weren't going to become a snake's meal either.

I had shuffled my way along the full length of the twelve-metre transportable and only had a few inches to go. With not even enough room to roll over, all I could do was blindly reach between the beams and hope the pup was close enough to grasp. Finally, I felt one little velvety foot and managed to wriggle the body connected to the foot into the palm of my hand. Mission accomplished, I started the backwards shuffle with my precious little cargo.

This wasn't my first dive under the old rooms. It used to be my job as the smallest and skinniest of the family to retrieve any stashed pups if we had litters when I was a kid. I could fit in the small gap quite easily, collect a few pups and be dragged out by my feet, hand them over, then be sent back in for the rest of them.

Though my girls very rarely have any trouble with whelping, I still like to monitor and hover, just in case. When they stop eating, I know the pups will be here the next day.

Once the first pup is born, I usually check every half hour or so, just to make sure things are progressing and everyone is doing well.

During my childhood, we had the token blue and red heelers that are so often found on rural Australian properties. Over the years we had a couple of litters and the last time, despite our best intentions and having set up the bitch with what we thought was a brilliant whelping box, we lost two pups overnight when they got stuck in the bedding. This had been in the back of my mind as I'd watched Chrissie prepare for her second litter, and my first with her, soon after I got her in 2014. Though she'd had access to a carpeted kennel, she'd instead chosen to dig a hole in the dirt nearby. I'd accepted that Chrissie had more experience in these matters than I did so I'd let nature take its course.

Watching her with her beautiful litter of eight pups I realised how clever that natural system is. By digging a hole for the pups to be whelped in, they all stayed huddled in the centre, keeping each other warm and preventing any from straying and getting separated. Chrissie was easily able to curl around the pups to feed them without squashing any outliers. The soil absorbed what remained of the birth that Chrissie didn't clean up herself, and the pups' immune systems were strengthened through the natural bacteria in the soil. Ground whelping also made it easier to cool the pups if the temperatures got too hot. We could dampen the soil and help keep the pups comfortable until they reached the age when they could move around and regulate their own temperatures.

There are many different whelping set-ups and each has its own risks and benefits. Ground whelping seems to work for us.

*

My original plan when I got my dogs was to have all girls and castrate any males. I had no intention of getting into the breeding world, but with the arrival of that first inherited litter of Chrissie's my views changed. I soon discovered a love of watching pups develop into their own little characters, changing from helpless newborns to rambunctious ratbags, ready to take on the world. Seeing Jinx's natural talent shine through, just like her mother's, made me appreciate the benefits of being able to continue my lines, breeding dogs who I knew would suit my work and world. Just, preferably one litter at a time …

*

I rounded the corner to the dog kennels and confronted seventeen eight-week-old kelpie pups running my way at full pelt. Sighing, I came to an abrupt halt. Pups score: 1; puppy pen renovations: 0.

I was currently in a battle of wills with these gorgeous little monsters, trying to keep them penned up while they did their best to get out. Obviously, I was losing.

I hadn't intended to have so many pups on the ground at once. I'm the first to admit accidents happen. In this instance, while I was celebrating the successful joining of my dogs Impulse (a dog I had bred) and Diamond, I unwisely turned my back on the resident Casanova, Mr Sinner, who took full advantage of my slip and had his way with beautiful old red-and-tan Tulli. I had picked Sinner up from Peter Barr during my last road trip and had bought Tulli as an experienced dog from Neil McDonald and his wife, Helen. Both dogs were great workers … but I hadn't intended to breed them together at this point.

I consoled myself like this:

'Surely Diamond and Tulli won't both get pregnant.'

They did.

'Okay, but surely they won't both have big litters …'

Of course, they did.

Diamond had a litter of nine beautiful black-and-tan pups and a few days later Tulli had eight gorgeous red-and-tan pups. The colour difference was a blessing and the only way we could tell the pups apart once they started exploring. Diamond and Tulli were incredible mums, neither being overly protective of their brood, and once the pups started mingling, they didn't mind which pups latched on for a feed.

Due to our mustering and other work commitments, I wasn't able to get the pups down to Perth and on their way to their new owners when they were eight weeks old, which is the practice I prefer. Instead, I kept them at home until twelve weeks. To say those extra few weeks were hectic would be an understatement. They were soon relocated from the house yard to a makeshift pen near the big dog kennels in a bid to save the last of the homestead garden and my mother's sanity. There they were incorporated into the big dog camp, learning important life skills such as communal feeding and interacting with the pack.

Any visits to the dog pen had to be strategically timed because you would undoubtedly require a shower after fending off the full contingent of wriggling, excited kids. Phil, originally from Queensland, had not long started with us on the station as a full-time employee and was often left holding the fort at home while we were at stock camp or working cattle in the yards. He would come back from a visit to the puppies completely covered in mud, dust and puppy licks, with a grin a mile wide. I'm sure the pups are what kept him with us for the next three years.

As full on and fun as it was to have such a large number of pups underfoot, there was definitely some relief for all when it was time to finally head south with them, ready for their new homes. We felt (and the place looked) like we'd survived a kelpie cyclone ... just.

*

It's almost a given on our property now that anyone who works or visits would do well to love dogs. Upon arriving, visitors are usually greeted by at least one maremma guardian dog (thanks Angel) and up to two or three kelpies. If they time it right, there may also be a litter of pups demanding their attention. Our pups are generally known as time-wasters. We spend as much time as we can with them between jobs, letting them out to run around underfoot during smoko and sitting with them on the lawn after knock-off. The puppy pen is located out the front of our homestead and they soon get used to all manner of vehicles, people and other dogs driving past. I believe this early socialisation is critically important for the pups' development, resulting in young dogs who are confident, brave and comfortable in a range of situations. It holds them in very good stead when it's time to head off to their new homes, and the most common feedback I get is how well adjusted the pups are. I've learnt over time and through my own experiences with buying young pups, just how important it is to get that start right.

I won't lie, sending pups off to their new homes can be very bitter-sweet. The hardest part is bundling those trusting little souls into a crate, often on their own, for a flight across the country and hoping that everything you have done in the eight weeks leading up to this moment will be enough. There is no way to explain to them that the trip is short, that you've done everything you can to ensure their safety, and that there is someone excitedly waiting at the other end to meet them. All I can do is hope that time passes quickly on the trip and keep my phone close, waiting for news of their arrival: 'I've just picked my pup up from the airport and, oh gosh, she is perfect! Thank you so much!'

My first trip to the airport found me sitting in my ute in tears as I watched the small face peering back at me from the crate disappear around the terminal building. Now I try to keep one of my own dogs waiting for me back at my ute. I can hold them close for my own comfort as I watch those uncertain eyes disappear towards their future.

Not all of the pups I select to keep from a litter end up staying with me long term. Most pups I usually sell at around eight months of age, after I have had a chance to assess their work style and test our bond. It's important to see first-hand what I am breeding, so I try to retain a pup from each litter, even if only till they have started showing interest in working.

One of the main reasons I don't retain many pups is because it usually means I have to shift on an already established dog to make room for a new one. I have reached a point with my team where I don't want to let any of my older dogs go. As much as I would love to keep every pup I raise, my limit is around twelve dogs. This gives me two teams of four working dogs, two young ones coming on and two in the wings for maternity leave and injuries and some semblance of sanity. I've had more dogs than this at times and it can get pretty hectic. I've had fewer and, though they do better for the regular, consistent work, we can be left short-handed very quickly. But every now and then a special pup wriggles its way into my team and stays there, learning alongside me on this journey we call life.

*

Appreciating dogs for their strengths and turning a perceived weakness into a positive is something I hadn't really considered until I met a dog handler with a refreshing outlook on life.

Diego and Strych were about two years old when I decided they didn't really fit in my team or with me anymore. Both had what I perceived as faults that drove me nuts. They were two of my first pups, and my lack of experience was very likely the reason for these 'faults', but I decided I'd had enough and it was time to move them on. I was approached by a man who had started managing another station in the district and was looking for a couple of extra dogs to help out his current team of two. So Diego and Strych headed across to live life close to the coast.

Strych could be a bit hot in the head; he was a busy thinker who could end up overheating himself in short order. He would get lost on a mob easily and 'boomerang' back to me constantly, wasting precious energy and taxing his stamina. All of these issues were an indication that he lacked confidence, most likely a product of my inexperience as a trainer.

Diego was a stronger pup, with plenty of strength but very little appreciation for the direction I wanted the stock to go in. What he lacked in finesse he made up for in exuberance. The final straw for me was his habit of 'shouldering' cattle (cutting in towards their shoulders) when they broke into a run, instead of getting around in front of them properly for a 'clean block'. Shouldering caused stock to jam the proverbial foot on the accelerator, and if there was a fence nearby, they'd be over it in a heartbeat with Diego encouraging them on.

I explained my issues to their new owner as he calmly took the boys.

'Let's just see how we go,' he said.

A few months later I rang up to see how they were all getting on.

'They are brilliant! I've been using them to muster in these feral cattle who hide in the tree line. They haven't been caught for a few years but we are getting a win on them.

'Diego doesn't lack any strength. He doesn't bark anymore and he'll bite hard when they need it. He'll stay out on those cattle as long as he needs to get a bend on them with my old girl.

'Strych has been renamed Striker and he's great. He casts out really wide with the others then returns to me before he heads back out again. It's good because I can just follow him back out to where the mob is and help the dogs.'

The new owner's appreciation of these dogs for their strengths, and turning what I saw as weaknesses into positives, was such a refreshing attitude. Instead of berating or holding things against the dogs, aiming for perfection, he just worked out how to use their idiosyncrasies to his advantage. He was also very open-minded and willing to learn new ways of doing things, a trait I admire and respect hugely. Little does he know, but this man had a big influence on me in the short time we knew each other.

When we caught up a year or so later, I learnt that Striker had got lost while out working and wasn't found for near on six weeks. How he survived that long and avoided all the 1080 wild dog baits we will never know, but he kept a very close shadow to his boss once he was home again. What melted my heart was hearing that the boys recognised my ute as I drove up to their new home and grew excited the closer I got. That they still remembered me after all that time, and fondly at that, made the reunion all the more bitter-sweet.

*

Although most stock-dog handlers seem to look for the elusive allrounder, I've learnt to appreciate having a balance of complementing strengths and styles in my team rather than chasing perfection. I now try to allow a dog to excel where their particular talent lies while still learning how to work all areas and situations. When I head out on a job, I select a team I know will have all areas covered between them and where one dog falls short, another is able to step up.

Over the years, I've had some very talented dogs pass through my team and I've learnt something from each and every one of them.

Chapter Twelve

The Start of the Storm

'If you can't see it, they can't eat it.'

– Unknown

Early 2017 had delivered some decent rain to the station but it had all fallen in the space of a month before the tap had shut off and winter passed with barely a drop. This wasn't a huge cause for concern, we had a run of average seasons behind us that were holding the cattle and the country in good stead. But throughout the summer of 2018, our precious wet season didn't arrive. That's not quite true. We did receive 36 millimetres from one storm in February that fell so hard and fast it did little more than turn our roads into waterways and disappear down the rivers. It doesn't matter how much lands in our rain gauge; if the rain doesn't have a chance to soak into the ground, it isn't effective.

We swung into mustering early in 2018 but were happy to stop when some winter rain fell, putting a bit of green feed back around the station. Sadly, that winter feed acted like a Band-Aid, hiding the continuing effects of the previous dry eighteen months. It kicked the grass along, but our subsoil moisture wasn't there to keep it going, and by late 2018, the feed and condition of our cattle started to fall away sharply.

Unfortunately, the previous run of good seasons had allowed our cattle numbers to increase and, by late 2018, as we finished the mustering lap, we recognised we needed to get the numbers back down. We made the call to cull a line of cows but with the majority being wet (raising a calf), pregnant or both, we rolled the dice and decided to hold them over the summer months. Surely this summer would deliver the rain we needed. It didn't.

Summer rains proved elusive yet again and by March of 2019, we had given up hope of receiving anything significant and started bringing our cattle in to reduce numbers. We mustered the northern part of the property first, leaving only our best breeding cows, pregnant cows and the smallest calves in the area and pulling everything else off. Weaners and larger calves were put on to specially formulated pellets and quality hay back at the homestead yards, while everything else that was potentially saleable was trucked south to the farm by

Dad. Murray had taken over management of our farms, plural now, as we had purchased half of the farm next door when the opportunity arose. Del's dad, Colin, purchased the other half which adjoined his place, essentially securing three farms in the family which could be jointly managed together. The timing of this expansion turned out to be pretty opportune.

We had just finished clearing out the northern end of the property when I received a call from the State Emergency Service in Onslow. Apparently Cyclone Veronica was barrelling our way and the prediction was for up to 400 millimetres of rain over this area. Even the potential for destructive winds and floods couldn't dampen our excitement about the forecasted rain. We made some preparations, pulling down old buildings that the resident white ants had left in a less than sturdy state; we didn't want sheets of iron flying around the place. Maybe that was where we went wrong. The golden rule if you want rain is to act as though it's not coming, like putting washing on the line, distributing mineral lick that ideally stays dry and pulling the tarp off your haystack. Nothing sensible like pulling down a dilapidated old building. All we got from Veronica was strong winds, dust storms and a few spits of rain while she stalled to the north, creating havoc over Port Hedland and surrounding stations, dumping her payload of moisture on them before trailing inland, leaving us high and dry once again. The disappointment was a hard blow to take.

*

While the farm essentially became a holding paddock for the station, with everything older than a weaner that was able to travel arriving there, at the station we were feeding hundreds of calves and weaners in the homestead yards and the small surrounding paddocks. With so many cattle living in close confines, the flies became unbearable. The yard rails would be coloured black with the buzzing insects, which shifted and moved around as you climbed through them. The only saving grace at this point was that they weren't biting flies.

In one of our paddocks close to the yards, a pattern was emerging that wasn't good. We were losing a weaner every couple of nights to dingoes. The weaners were easy prey without the protection of their mothers, and though most survived the initial attack, turning up the next day at the trough, they eventually had to be euthanised due to the severity of their injuries.

I put a few older cows out with the weaners to try and afford the young cattle some protection. We made special frames to put around the pellet feeders so the weaners could access the feed without the cows gutsing it all, much to the cows' disgust. They could hold on foraging the shrubs in the paddock and eating the hay; the kids couldn't. The smaller weaners were also fed specially formulated pellets and quality oaten hay in the yards to supplement the milk they weren't receiving from mum. Some hadn't been receiving it for a while and it showed in their rough coats and big pot bellies.

It was after putting down another weaner that I finally decided if there was ever a time to get a maremma guardian dog, it was now. I should have looked for an older, already working maremma that could start guarding our weaners in the paddock in a matter of weeks, but that epiphany was still a while away. Instead, I got what at first glance looked like two gorgeous, fluffy, oversized white poodles.

From the moment our two new eight-week-old maremma pups arrived from Penny in Queensland (who had introduced me to maremmas four years earlier), I was smitten. Already the size of a six-month-old kelpie, the siblings Rafael and Angel looked extremely out of place in the Pilbara landscape. Despite all temptation, they were not allowed near the house, instead settling into their makeshift kennel, a decommissioned stock crate that doubled as our hayshed's back wall.

On the advice of Penny, we selected three two-week-old calves named Caesar (because he had been born via caesarean), Julius and Brutus (continuing the theme) from our poddy mob to live with them, so the bonding could begin. Twice a day we would feed the calves and visit the pups, letting them out to run around and explore nearby. Every time we visited, I would have a kelpie or two in tow, so the pups soon recognised that the kelpies were part of the show and not a threat. This maybe

Working on the theory that if you can't make the fence dog proof, make the dogs fence proof. Angel and Rafael.

worked a little too well, as I'm sure Rafael still gets more excited to see the other dogs than me.

It wasn't long before the pups and calves grew used to each other's company and their interactions fascinated me. Watching the maremmas develop their natural instinct to bond, guard and protect was amazing; they were working dogs of a completely new style to anything I had seen before. The calves became comfortable having the pups underfoot, tumbling into and around them in the hay. The pups got smart to hoofs and learnt to keep precious paws and tails safe from a careless step.

As the pups grew and settled into their new role on the station, we shifted the party of five into a larger pen in the cattle yards and bumped their little mob up with a few more calves. Over time, we kept increasing the number of calves in the mob until the dogs were living out in our 'weaner pen' with close to 200 bovine friends.

It was at this point I realised trying to make our fence maremma-proof was futile without extensive new fencing materials, so I tried the ingenious idea of making the maremma's fence-proof. This involved a triangle collar made out of light polypipe, tied together with twine. It did work for a time, preventing the pups from squeezing underneath the fence or through any gaps while the collars remained in place. What I didn't allow for was the play factor of two pups. Soon enough, over the course of a few nights the collars were pulled apart and left scattered around the yard. But they had done the job. The pups had learnt where their mob was and soon didn't stray too far. Or at least, Rafael didn't.

While Rafe (Rafael's nickname) lived with the weaners, Angel discovered the homestead and decided she wasn't really cut out for yard work. She is what I refer to as my 'failed guardian', though in all honesty it seems she just decided she wanted a different role.

Maremmas are used in a range of guardian roles including with cattle, horses, sheep, goats, chooks, penguins (as shown in the movie *Oddball*, inspired by real events), people and property. Though I would have loved for Angel to help Rafe in the intended purpose of guarding our young stock, I wasn't overly surprised that the uncoordinated and slight-of-frame girl preferred the softer homestead lifestyle. She still followed us up the yards and visited with her brother, usually to tumble around the yards in play with him, blocking gateways and scattering mobs, both completely oblivious to the chaos and exasperation left in their wake. But she took her duties at the homestead very seriously. If you wandered out in the night and happened upon a sleeping Angel, she would jump up and take off barking into the distance like she had been caught slacking off and had to redeem herself with noise. No amount of calling or cajoling would settle her ruffled feathers as she resumed her duties, usually in the opposite direction of the kangaroos happily keeping our lawn trimmed around her.

*

It was after we finished the north end and headed out to the eastern side of the station that I finally made the call we'd never made before on Glen Florrie. We would try and clear this entire side of the station. Every animal we mustered in would be pulled off the country, our best breeding cows included. Cattle were doing it so tough it was the only option we seemed to have left.

We soon established a system that worked well. If we finished the muster early in the day, we would leave the stock undisturbed for the afternoon to rest and recover before we loaded them onto the truck the next morning to head back to the main homestead yards. We would draft off the younger and stronger stock to be loaded on the top deck of the two-decker cattle crates while the older cattle travelled on the bottom deck to save them the effort of climbing up the ramp. Our station tracks were soon billowing with fine clouds of bull dust as the tyres kept rolling back and forth. Machinery maintenance was put on hold as we focused on getting stock to feed.

It wasn't just the station truck bringing cattle into the yards that was kept busy. Dad must have felt like he was practically living full-time in his Kenworth as he loaded cattle from the yards off the property. Considering most cattle were heading to our farm 1200 kilometres to the south, the turnaround time was a minimum of 48 hours before he could reload again, without allowing time for maintenance or a decent sleep. There were times when he couldn't keep up with the numbers we had waiting to move, so outside trucks were contracted to shift the extra loads of cattle. This was how I met my partner, Adam.

An electrician by trade, Adam had been driving trucks shifting general freight and oversized loads for the better part of seven years before he decided to try his hand at carting cattle. What a year to start. The majority of the cattle being moved in 2019 from this area were drought affected, requiring extra care and preparation to get them safely to their destination, usually many hours away. We were doing everything we could for our cattle before they left the station to make their trip easier, providing electrolytes and extra feed to help shore up their energy reserves, and in the hours leading up to loading on the truck, keeping them off water so they didn't load up with a full belly of liquid. They were also given electrolytes at the receiving end of the trip to help them recover. These recommended practices helped, but sometimes wet weather during the journey or other unplanned delays slowed everything down and you'd feel for the girls as they would unload exhausted at the other end.

Markets were hard to find for 'store' cattle, cattle who were in poor condition, and not 'finished', or suitable for the abattoir. That end wasn't what we wanted for our breeder cows, at any rate, but at this point we didn't have many options left. The farm was already running over capacity, with Murray remarking over one phone call that receiving more cattle from the station was 'his least favourite form of torture'. As often seems to happen, when the station has a dry stint, so does the farm. Buying in hay and pellets to feed cattle until markets could be found for them was, in some cases, all we could do. Agistment was elusive while southern Western Australia was waiting for rain to kick the grass along, and we weren't the only ones in drought scrambling to get our stock onto feed. With the dry run being felt across a number of stations, any available agistment was in high demand. Cyclone Veronica had delivered some relief to properties in her path but plenty of the northwest was still in a world of pain and around us was one of the worst areas.

Even at this dark time, somehow we were lucky. Each time we felt we had nowhere to turn, a new door would open. We were unbelievably fortunate to have offers of agistment, hay, free lease country and help from friends and family right across the state. It was humbling to recognise the close network we had supporting us through this drought, and I hope that one day I get a chance to return this generosity and pay it forward.

*

It was while mustering our eastern country that I faced another heartbreak I didn't see coming.

Jinx, now five years old, was almost human in her personality. A pint-sized bundle of energy, she spent half her life leaping from vehicle to person, bouncing on her back legs like a pogo stick.

Her natural herding skills only improved with age; she worked all areas of the mob, keeping the tail going during long musters and turning an animal with a sharp nose bite when she needed to. She loved tagging along in the buggy or riding front and centre on the bike. One of the most common phrases heard around the station during her reign was 'Jinx! Get in the back!' as her head sneaked in under your arm to get closer to the action, or your vision turned red as she wormed her way onto your lap while you were driving the bull wagon.

Jinx gave me two beautiful litters of pups over the years, and they have made homes for themselves across Australia, excelling both as stock dogs and much-loved pets. As with her mother, Chrissie, Jinx preferred the company of people to dogs. She'd squeeze in around the feed bowl, growling constantly as she shovelled biscuits into her mouth till her cheeks looked like a chipmunk's, then run a few metres away and spit them out and eat them steadily on her own. She had a certain few males she would tolerate, but everyone else got the cold shoulder and an upturned lip. Every human, however, was met with joy and a complete disregard for personal space. She had more than her share of confidence and total belief that everyone loved her, which they always did in the end, even if they tried to resist.

Jinx had been on long maternity leave while recovering from hypocalcaemia complications brought on during her second litter of pups, so she hadn't been working much in recent weeks. But I still had her out at stock camp with us so she could be part of the action. It had been a long day for all, walking the cattle in from fifteen kilometres away to the portable set of yards we had set up. As I headed out to tail in the last mob of twelve head of stragglers, I called past the camp and picked up Jinx. I didn't need her, the other dogs were more than capable of getting the job done, but she had been patiently sitting in the dogs' cages on my ute while all the fun happened around her and was keen to get out. I also wanted to ease her back into work and see how she handled it. What I wouldn't do to go back and change that fatal decision.

The dogs and I found the cattle, gathered them together and headed back to where the main mob waited. I rode up front on the bike, once the cattle had settled, leaving the dogs working to draw them along behind me. It was then that I heard Jasper's distinctive bark followed by a kerfuffle and a yelp from behind the mob. My best guess as to what happened is that a cleanskin cow unused to the kelpies turned back on the dogs to protect her calf, and Jasper met her challenge. Jinx would have used this cue to fly in from the side and deliver a quick bite, as was her style. The problem with Jinx's method was often the situation had changed by the time she got there and she would end up underfoot but was still quick or lucky enough to dodge the danger. There is no denying her inherited bravery could be at the price of self-preservation, something that had caused me many grey hairs over the years. This time, her luck didn't hold.

I did a quick check when I heard the yelp but all dogs were present and seemingly intact and happy, so I chalked it up to a light warning blow and we continued on. Jinx would come and hop on and off the bike. She didn't seem to be able to settle but wasn't showing any signs of lameness. Something didn't seem right, though, so first chance I had, I took her back up to the ute and made sure she had plenty of water and could rest. My hope was she just felt a bit fatigued after the exercise.

I scooted back to the mob, yarding up the cattle with the crew before heading back to the ute to check on Jinx again. When I opened the cage door, she greeted me with a muted version of her normal sass, and as I lifted her from the cage, I could feed a sponginess over the left side of her ribcage. My heart lurched into my throat as I ran my hands all over her body for any other signs of injury and checked her gums. Pale gums, laboured breathing and the foamy swelling over her ribs was telling me a story I didn't want to hear.

I raced her over to our camp on the quad bike, running through options in my head. I had none. There was no way

I could get her to medical help in time if what I suspected was true. Our homestead was three hours away, let alone a vet clinic, and daylight was disappearing fast. All I could do was try to make her as comfortable as possible, stay close and pray for a miracle.

One of our stockmen, Steve, came over to see if he could help.

'Can you please get the rifle out of the truck?' My voice was quiet as I cradled Jinx close.

Steve startled. 'It hasn't got to that point, has it?'

'Not yet but if it does, I want to be ready to save her from the pain.'

Deep down, I already knew how this was going to end. I wanted every last second I could have with my girl. I talked to her softly and cradled her close. She kept nuzzling my hand and slowly wagging her tail, offering me the comfort I was trying to give her. In the end, before Steve could return with the gun, Jinx's punctured lungs gave out and she took her last breath. There, in the dust, I sobbed my goodbyes, as Jinx left me to join her mother, watching over us from above.

I buried Jinx out near our stock camp, in a creek line with a gorgeous river gum standing tall and proud above the grave. Her name and dates are etched into the tree's bark, recalling an incredible friend whose spirit is as bright in memory as it was in life. A once-in-a lifetime dog who deserved more than the short lifetime she had.

Jinx's final resting place.

*

There is no denying that the work we ask our dogs to do is often dangerous and unpredictable. Despite that, these high-drive dogs live for the chance to work livestock. Win their hearts, earn their respect and these amazing animals will give us their all. Accidents happen. Sometimes all it takes is a slight misstep to turn an ordinary working day into one you forever wish you could go back and relive differently. My dogs don't want to be wrapped in cotton wool but there are situations that I recognise now as too risky, when the cost isn't worth the gain, and the dogs are kept away to work another day. They are worth more to me than one more cow in the yards ever will be.

Chapter Thirteen

Predators and Predation

'A kelpie musters, a dingo menaces.'

— Brian Dray, cattle producer

My maremma pups were growing quickly but they were still just that, pups, and with Angel having taken herself off yard duties, Rafe was facing an impossible situation. So once again I called Penny, who was in the process of destocking her property in Queensland, also due to drought. As unfortunate as that was, it meant she had a mature maremma dog available for me.

The day I picked up Ringer still haunts me. Due to an airline protocol of adult dogs not being transported with a collar on, I collected a fully grown male maremma, who had been bred to guard and protect, with no idea of who I was, at the airport, with no easy means of getting him out of his crate and into my ute. Originally I had planned to ask my brother to pick Ringer up, but Murray was hobbling around on crutches after a fall from his horse so I thought better of that. I managed to get Ringer up into my dog box, though it was touch and go for a minute while I lifted the great lump up like a puppy. I was seriously wondering how I would explain things to security if Ringer got loose at 9pm in the middle of Perth Airport. What I also soon realised was my cages, designed for the now seemingly quite small kelpies, were not adequate for a full-sized maremma. Luckily Ringer obliged by lying down for most of the long 1350-kilometre trip home.

Once we got back to the station, I put Ringer with three small weaners in one of the smaller yards we had used for the pups. He soon showed me how inept my pen-building skills were, scaling the fence in a way the pups couldn't. I had put a collar on him and attached a rope so I could catch him again if necessary, but after coralling him for a third time with no more success, I gave him his freedom. He kept the collar and rope on a little longer till he finally worked out how to slip them over his head. Seems the extra thick coat of maremmas has more uses than just insulating them against the sun. It also makes it very hard to fit a collar snugly.

Ringer soon picked up his role as protector of the weaners. Rafe, now close to six months old and as tall as Ringer, was more than a little put out at the new male on the block. Ringer never instigated the blues, but when Rafe got too full of himself and challenged Ringer, he wouldn't back down either. Over time and a few war wounds, mainly sustained by Rafe, they settled their differences and learnt to get along. They each took on a different mob of weaners, though they sometimes shared and swapped too. The water point for the weaner paddock was at our house yards, so the dogs would return each day as the weaners came in for a drink. One evening I put a tracking collar on Rafe and found he was covering over fifteen kilometres in the night, scouting and protecting his mob. No wonder he and Ringer would spend the majority of the day sleeping with the calves in the shade of the yard trees.

*

One of the most fascinating aspects of introducing maremmas to our property has been watching the interactions of working dogs of an entirely different persuasion with our livestock. When we bring in a new mob of cattle to the yards, Ringer is quick to recognise the cattle are strangers and tears around, barking up a storm. Once I figure out how to teach him where to bark more strategically, our yards-ups will become a lot easier. But I've learnt to appreciate this is part of the process.

For the first few days, as the guardian dogs move through and around the new mob, they sporadically bark and run into the cattle, who react accordingly and at times return the chase, minus the bark. Angel, in particular, loves this game. Generally, by the third day, the cattle pay the maremmas little to no heed as they wander close by, instead keeping their focus on the kelpie sitting over yonder at the fence line. It's the perfect example of how livestock read intent and just how big an influence our body language can be.

In the time we've had the maremmas, we have seen the effects of only one dingo attack on the weaners they were guarding. Without being there to know what happened, it is hard to say whether the dogs saved the calf's life by interrupting the attack and limiting the damage to something survivable, or if they were absent when it happened and the weaner was lucky.

Dingoes cop a hard rap, especially from livestock producers. Not necessarily without fair reason. My great-grandad, Robert Lukis, was forced to walk off his property in October 1945, due in large part to the decimation of his sheep by dingoes. The senseless massacring of hundreds of sheep, jammed into the corners of paddocks, helpless and unable to escape, would have been heartbreaking. After years spent hunting the much more mobile and athletic kangaroos, sheep must have provided the dingoes with novel and easy prey. Even though cattle are not as vulnerable as sheep, dingoes have proved themselves deadly predators by taking young calves and, in hard times, preying on weaners and adult cattle in poor condition.

Great-grandad Lukis had a grudging respect for the cunning of the dingo predator, despite the depredations. My grandma recalls the story of a black dingo that he spent years in a battle of wills with. The dingo had at one point been caught in a trap and had lost a toe, making its tracks very distinctive. No matter how Rob set up his own traps, the black dog remained elusive, outsmarting him at every turn. Rob even placed a significant bounty on the dog's head if anyone was able to capture it but, to Grandma's knowledge, the dog was never caught.

Some people say the dingo is not native to Australia. It is believed that dingoes arrived in Australia some 3500 years ago and I would argue that it is a long time to have lived in a country and still not be considered a native. It is understandable that, through interbreeding with wild dogs, the natural behaviour of the dingo has been affected, the balance torn askew, and numbers have increased alongside water availability and more prevalent prey. A few years ago, Murdoch University took DNA samples from dogs that had been trapped or shot on properties to test how much dingo DNA was present. On our property, the results came back nearly 100 per cent dingo on all samples sent in, with northern and western Australia showing the largest concentration of purebred dingoes in Australia. Where there is evidence of large domestic dogs interbreeding with dingoes, the need for more drastic control measures like aerial baiting and 'doggers' (people employed specifically for managing wild dog numbers) is understandable. We still do perimeter baiting on our property out of respect for our neighbours, appreciating that dingoes can travel over a hundred kilometres into new territory once they reach maturity. But with the incorporation of working dogs into our operation, we limit this control method to areas we don't often frequent.

I used to hate dingoes with a passion rivalling my grandmother's. I've lost count of the number of calves we have doctored, hand-raised and lost over the years to infections and injuries sustained during a dingo attack – calves coaxed back from dehydration and illness only to be lost to predators as soon as they have left the safety of the poddy pens.

Besides the emotional loss of pets, there is a huge economic loss experienced by the Australian pastoral industry each year through livestock deaths as well as sustained injuries reducing the value of the livestock. But, as a friend recently pointed out to me, dingoes aren't the problem, livestock predation is. And I think that's an important way to look at it.

The susceptibility of livestock to dingo predation can also be caused by poor land management. This might be a tough pill to swallow. Droughts happen, there is no getting around that fact, especially in Australia. If we don't make the tough calls early, our cattle end up in poor condition, making them easy targets for a savvy hunter. It's not just drought, though. Even in the good seasons, it can be easy to overstock country while the rains are generous and the feed seems abundant, with only a focus on the cattle's requirements. Studies over the years looking into the effect of dingoes on domestic livestock have shown that the incidence of calf predation by dingoes can be significantly reduced if their preferred wildlife prey is available. So it stands to reason we can reduce predation vulnerability if we manage our country in a way that supports the local wildlife alongside our livestock, keeping the biodiversity healthy and our cattle strong, through the good times and bad. Easier said than done, perhaps, but a strategy I am passionate about pursuing through education and regeneration.

*

There is no black and white, especially in nature. Everything is entwined and it all depends which side of the window you are looking from as to what you see. When we watch a David Attenborough documentary, if we are following a pack of lions and know how important it is for the lioness to make the kill so she can feed her cubs, we are praying she'll succeed in bringing the antelope down so her cubs won't go hungry. But if we have been following the journey of the antelope and have just watched that young calf experience its first few weeks of life, we are on the edge of our seats hoping against hope it can escape the hunter. Dingoes, like lions and wolves, are pursuit hunters. The quick movements of their prey startling and running can stimulate their instincts to attack.

These same instincts are often used by working-dog handlers to switch on and to draw out the desire to work in slower developing dogs. The excitement of fast-moving animals, especially sheep or goats, can be the start of a great working dog's career. Or the end of it, if it isn't managed correctly. This strong instinct can lead to the surplus killing of livestock by wild dogs, dingoes and unrestrained working and town dogs. This is why it is so important that working dogs be supervised or restrained when not working stock. Left to their own devices, the instincts we value in working dogs can lead them to strife. It's the responsibility of all dog owners, working and pet, to ensure this doesn't happen. For the dogs' sake as well as that of the livestock they might find.

The benefits of working cows and calves with dogs was something I'd had difficulty explaining until I was able to spend time on a property outside of Darwin with Spud Thomas. Spud has an incredible wealth of knowledge when it comes to behaviour in both dogs and cattle, and he was able to show me what I was ultimately trying to achieve with our cows and why.

On this one day we were out checking a mob of cows that were in the middle of a calf drop. As we moved around them, calves that had been out playing headed into the safety of the main mob. Cows with young at foot slowly stood them up and walked in with their calves tucked in safe at their sides. If calves ended up adrift of the herd, Spud allowed a couple of his working dogs to move up on them and gently shift them in the right direction until they realised where safety lay. He was teaching them how to protect themselves against predators, through the use of working dogs. It doesn't happen overnight. As Spud said, 'The process, from starting on cows that haven't had dogs before to calm, soft, well-educated animals, takes a minimum of three years initially, and they will keep improving, till after five to six years, you'll be doing things initially thought to be impossible.'

Most people who have handled cows and calves with dogs will have seen over-protective cows who work themselves up into a fury, hurtling around in a frantic, well-intentioned effort to defend their calves. But these are actually the calves most likely to get taken by wild dogs. The cow knocks her calf over, stands on it as she tries to guard it or leaves it vulnerable while trying to chase off the threat. This is exactly what the predators are hoping will happen, especially if they are working in a pack. The abandoned, bruised or injured calf is easy prey for a well-coordinated attack. If that calf is able to stay tucked in next to mum while mum stays calm and close, predatory dogs don't stand the same chance of an easy feed.

As breeders, our intention isn't to teach our cows that dogs aren't dangerous, but to train the fear and panic out of the situation by teaching them how to handle that kind of threat. We can start this process when they are weaners.

The majority of my experience is with Brahman cattle, which are notoriously curious, especially weaners (teenagers). They love nothing better than sniffing, licking, chewing, playing with everything new and interesting. Potential predators provide the same exciting discovery, encouraging young stock to leave the safety of the herd to investigate further. All it takes is one well-placed bite that, even if it doesn't prove immediately fatal, can bleed, fester and weaken the calf with infection for a predator meal later.

This is where educating stock with dogs can really prepare stock against predation. I would rather those weaners express their curiosity with my working dogs, who won't injure them, but will teach them a predator is dangerous and to be respected, preferably with distance. The weaners also learn at the same time to stay together as a mob, that there is protection in numbers, and not to spook and rush at any little sound. They learn how to flow through yards and gateways and how to block up and walk when asked: the basic education that all stock should learn. A flow-on from this is learning how to handle stress and different situations they haven't experienced before. This early education will stay with them through life and will be passed on to future generations, who learn it at their mother's side.

Utilising working dogs to educate our cattle has been our first step towards mitigating predation on our property. Though reducing predator pressure wasn't my original reason for getting a team of working dogs, it has been one of the unexpected benefits, both for the welfare of the cattle and for us financially – though that is hard to measure.

*

I don't claim to know what the answer is when it comes to dingoes and predation on livestock. Far from it. I don't think there is an elusive silver bullet. I just know that I can't consider the ecosystem as a whole without including the dingo as part of that. My hope is to find ways we can learn to live together a little more harmoniously. I do believe the maremmas have been a valuable inclusion into our management system. I hope to soon expand our maremma numbers and their range of protection across our property. As a non-lethal control method for stock protection against dingoes, it's one I want to explore further in our bid to live more harmoniously with the natural world. Not that it doesn't come with its own share of challenges ...

There are other complications to incorporating a new working-dog breed onto the property. As I write, Ringer is standing guard outside the kennel of Sass, one of my kelpie girls. Ringer is as adamant that he would be her perfect partner as I am that he wouldn't. Unfortunately, he has good reason to be optimistic as he's bested me before in this scenario. Nothing says accidental litter like a working–guardian dog cross. Sass had finally come in season and I had high hopes for the progeny she and Cruise, another of my male dogs, were going to produce. Unfortunately, Cruise was playing hard to get so we headed down to the yards where they could flirt while I pottered in the orchard. I hadn't forgotten about the maremmas but I figured I would keep an eye on them. It would be fine: those famous last words.

I looked up from shifting a hose and saw a clueless Cruise sitting nearby with no Sass in sight. There was also no Ringer and 30 minutes later, I still had not located them. When Sass did eventually show up, I was suspicious about what had occurred in that lost half hour and didn't want to take any chances, so plan B was hastily formed. It's the first time I have resorted to using a drug to avoid a litter but, with Sass being slight of frame and Ringer quite large, I didn't want to risk birthing complications. The horse had already bolted, as they say, but I was determined to catch it in the paddock. Except I couldn't.

Two months on, Sass had developed an udder and was showing every sign of pregnancy, which I was steadfastly denying. 'The drug is 99 per cent foolproof. She couldn't possibly be pregnant,' was the mantra I kept repeating to myself. Even when she started having contractions, I was still dead-set sure it was a phantom pregnancy, on the more extreme side, admittedly. One of our heelers had experienced regular phantom pregnancies when I was a kid, so I knew they could mimic a real pregnancy quite realistically. My denial continued until I crawled under the dusty schoolroom floor where Sass had dug a hole, and after a quick check over, had to accept that this was no phantom pregnancy. My fears of any pups being large were valid. With some help, Sass was able to whelp her little daughter and I couldn't help but smile at the beautiful blue-roan pup that had been so determined to greet the world; she beat all the odds.

That little pup, named Hush, grew into a gorgeous girl who lives a great life on a friend's sheep property, where she still hasn't decided whether she wants to herd the sheep or guard them. Ringer had the last laugh that time and despite the beautiful outcome, it's a cross I'm determined not to repeat.

Chapter Fourteen

The Devastation of Drought

**'I don't know how people manage a property without dogs.
I know I wouldn't be here still if it wasn't for them.'**
— Aticia Grey

In a brief gap between musters, we again hosted a Neil McDonald school on the property. At the time, it seemed hard to justify pulling up our mustering to take three days to learn about dog and stock handling. But it was an opportunity I had promised our crew we would provide for them and it was well worth it in the end. A great weekend of learning from one of the most entertaining trainers I know, catching up with friends who had travelled from all across the state for the school, and enjoying evenings around a fire. Even aside from the social aspect, it put the whole crew on to the same page when it came to stock handling and the rest of the season was spent practising our skills, encouraging each other to improve and tweaking our cattle-yard designs.

The helicopter company that provided the choppers for our musters also believed strongly in providing their pilots with opportunities to improve their cattle-handling skills, and that year they put their pilots through Neil McDonald's school. Aside from gaining a better understanding of cattle behaviour, it also allowed the pilots to understand and appreciate what we were doing with our dogs back down on the ground.

There was a muster in 2019 when it really hit home to me just how much influence the pilots have over the livestock we handle as ground crew. Mum and I were waiting on a large flat for the first mob of cattle to be brought out to us and we were feeling a little edgy. It was that moment of calm that usually preceded the storm. I had my dogs with me on the quad, ready to fan out and cover the mob, but considering the country we were mustering, with evidence that scrub bulls had mixed with our breeders, I was in no doubt things were about to get interesting. But when one of our regular pilots, Peter, brought the cattle trotting out to where we were waiting, the lead pulled up calmly, the mob settled like a herd of old dairy cows and we headed off up the road as if they'd done it a hundred times before. In that moment I realised just how much easier our work is on the ground when we have good stockmen/women handling the cattle well from the air.

As fortunate as I have been with everyone who's worked on the property, the crew of 2019 were something else. They experienced the worst of the place in drought but still saw the beauty too. The days were long, the conditions heartbreaking but everyone gave it their best and morale stayed high. For the most part.

After one particularly hard stint of back-to-back musters, dawn starts and late finishes, a mix-up in chopper dates had us pulling up suddenly and unexpectedly. It was a blessing in disguise. I hadn't realised just how exhausted we all were, with tempers running hot and tolerance low. As it coincided with the West Australian election, the crew all headed into town for a night off while I regrouped with Mum at home. It was a timely lesson for me to be more aware of the pressure and workload I was putting everyone under. We had been heading, already exhausted, into a scrubber muster with dangerous cattle in rough country, and asking more of a tired crew would have been a disaster in the making. As it was, one of our crew still sustained a serious injury when a scrub bull got the best of him and I shudder to think of how much worse it could have easily been.

By the time we finished our first mustering lap of the station, we needed to redo the early areas again. It had been slow going, shifting portable yards to each new spot, mustering smaller areas so we weren't asking the cattle to walk as far. At the end of the first day of our second lap, three realisations were dawning on me. One was that, considering the number of cattle that we had missed the first round now picked up in the second, we needed to re-evaluate our mustering strategy for covering large areas. The second was that with so many cattle being left behind, we couldn't estimate with any certainty how many stock were in an area. And thirdly, we wouldn't be able to bush any cattle back out to this area. I had been hoping to hold our core breeders on this northern country till the rains returned but I had to accept that the country couldn't hold the cattle it still had on it, let alone any more. We had no feed left, no spare paddocks and nowhere else to go. We had hit a fork in the road. I rang Murray on the satellite phone from stock camp after Mum and I had discussed our options, or lack of them. 'We can't bush cows back out here, Murray. I don't know where they are going to go but they can't stay on this country.'

One of the darkest times for me in the drought was having to watch our dry breeders (those without a calf at foot) load onto the trucks that would take them to the meatworks. They had done everything right but were the ones left paying the ultimate price for bad seasons, late decisions and a flooded cattle market. It nearly broke me. My only consolation was knowing not all our cattle were destined for this fate. We secured temporary agistment for a large number of our cows that were pregnant or with calves at foot. This eventually turned into a permanent home, as their good temperament shone through. We were also offered an area on a family's property to hold some of our core breeders, which would make all the difference in helping us get back on our feet when the drought finally broke.

I am a firm believer in the theory that we can only make the best decision we can with the information we have at the time. Even if it had rained the following week, that decision would have been the right one. Knowing it was the best call, not just for our cattle but for our country as well, helped me hold it together.

We shifted the majority of the cattle over the course of 2019, but it was impossible to move them all. Some were in a condition too poor to travel, others we never saw until after we had thought the area was clear. So our priority moved from shifting cattle to helping the ones that remained survive until it remembered how to rain again. We started up new water points to try and open up country that we hoped hadn't been as heavily grazed, but the best of the feed had already been eaten, by both the cattle and the feral donkeys whose numbers seemed impervious to the drought.

To add insult to injury, as the temperature heated up towards the end of the year lice started plaguing our remaining herds. Generally we don't have a worm or lice problem with our stock but when the cattle start getting too run-down, they become vulnerable to parasites. We gathered the animals up as they came into the water points using a simple set of basic trap yards, with my dogs collecting any stragglers so we could put them through the race and treat them for lice. Any calves or missed weaners were pulled off to be raised at home, and the cows we bushed again were supplemented heavily with a specially formulated high-energy mineral lick. We had been supplementing our cattle all along but with a standard mineral mix that didn't seem to be providing them with what they needed. Once we changed to the new lick, the high-protein content along with the other minerals in it helped the cattle process what low-nutrient feed they had available and, coupled with the easing of the lice burden, we saw the benefits within weeks. The cows' coats became shiny, their stride stronger, and as we watched the horizon for any sign of rain, we started to think we might just make it through this terrible time.

There was one bright light. What started as a tentative friendship between Adam and me as he continued to shift our cattle, along with many others in the west Pilbara region, in 2019, eventually blossomed into something more. Our first date was not your traditional 'wine and dine' in a restaurant. Instead, after meeting on the road at eleven o'clock at night, as I headed south to the farm and Adam was returning north, we spent what was left of the evening sharing stories over a few drinks on top of his empty stock crates. We sat under the most gorgeous blanket of stars we could have asked for and it felt fitting in a way. We both shared a love of trucks and the outback lifestyle, which would hold us in good stead for the future. It would be another year before Adam would move to the station with me and experience station life first-hand.

*

One of my grandma's childhood wishes was to enjoy a white Christmas with preferably a large number of her family alongside. Two years earlier, I had mentioned to Mum's side of the family that if we wanted to make this happen for Grandma, it should probably be soon, while she could still travel long distances overseas. Then the drought occurred. If there is ever a time you don't feel you can take a break, it's while things are looking bleak at home. But, as Murray pointed out, maybe it was the best time. We had done everything we could for the cattle we had left on both properties. Dad, handyman Phil and Murray's father-in-law, Colin, could hold the fort in our absence and, if we didn't go now, it might never happen. If only I had known my goodbye to Flora was to be my last.

Over the nearly seven years that she had been with me, Flora had won over every person who met her. She had more retirement homes lined up waiting for her than any dog could ever need. She nearly got early retirement in 2017 when she misstepped and tore her cruciate ligament while out working cattle after a muster. But I owed this girl more than I could ever repay, so after a successful surgery and recovery, she was soon back out doing what she loved in the paddocks.

Due to not knowing Flora's age, it was hard to pinpoint just what stage of life she was at. I made the decision to have her spayed, on advice it would eliminate chances of her developing associated cancers, so in 2018 she spent a wonderful three months over summer with my cousin Kristy, who, as a vet nurse, was more than qualified to look after her post-operation. Flora wasted no time in making herself part of the family. I would receive photos of her snuggled into the kids' beds, her floppy ears and brown eyes peering out from under the covers. I'd be regaled with stories of her guilting Kristy's husband, Russell, into shifting places on the couch when she found him in *her spot*. Her favourite pastime was stalking the chooks in the garden, eyeballing them through the fence and checking how securely the gate latch worked. After a few poultry incidents at home, when Flora hadn't been quite quick enough to leave the scene of the crime to avoid suspicion (she wandered past me with the poor victim still in her mouth), I had advised Kristy not to trust her any closer than that.

I have different retirement plans for all of my dogs, each one dependent on what I think will give them their best last years. For Flora, her work drive was always going to outreach her body's capability as she got older and I knew she would never be happy knowing there was work going on that she wasn't a part of. So she returned home to me for one final season before she would retire to my cousin's to spend her final days enjoying soft beds, the cool temperatures of the south and the kids' many loving pats. But she never got that retirement she so deserved.

On Christmas Day in 2019, Flora was bitten by a mulga snake, also known as a king brown. She was found by Dad and Phil out in the grass behind our coolroom, barely breathing. Her trademark floppy ear with its torn tip was swollen from the bite. We can only assume she had flushed it out while chasing lizards, a bad habit she had long practised. She had lived her last summer around the house in semi-retirement which, in the end, proved her downfall.

It was devastating to hear the news, for all of us. I wasn't ready to lose Flora, I don't think I ever would have been. But I realise now I was never going to feel I could do without her. She was irreplaceable, both in her work and her beautiful nature. She was the matriarch of my team and her loss will continue to be felt for many years to come.

*

Despite the loss of Flora, the timing of our Christmas trip was perfect. We arrived home a few short months before international travel came to a sudden halt in 2020. Though Grandma didn't get her white Christmas, it was still deliciously cold and beautifully festive in her favourite city in the world, Vienna, surrounded by her family. A trip to remember as we wonder when we'll see our offshore friends and family again.

Chapter Fifteen

The Heat of Winter

'There are three things guaranteed in life:
death, taxes and portable panels.'
– Aticia Grey

When your property spans nearly half a million acres, it's fair
to hope that at least some part of it will get decent rain during
the 'wet season'. The summer of 2019–2020 was long, hot and
disappointingly dry. The saving grace was our lack of stock.
Though we hadn't been able to fully destock, our numbers
were low enough that what little feed did come up from the
localised storms was enough to sustain the cattle we had left.
As the months passed, our hopes turned towards winter rain
to give us enough feed to see out the year. Cattle that had

been out on agistment were sold or shifted, while some of the heifers we desperately wanted to keep as replacement breeders came home. We were gambling that rain would surely fall soon, somewhere. In preparation for these heifers turning up, Mum and I decided to 'clean up' the country where they were going to be released. It had received enough rain over summer through isolated storms that the cattle we had missed during mustering the year before were fat. A number of these were sale cattle that didn't need to be eating what feed we did have on hand. We just had to get them in ...

I had decided that Mum and I could handle mustering the elusive straggler cattle on our own, with just the help of the dogs. The cattle were camping at the water troughs during the day, so we had to gather them together and walk towards each succeeding water trough till we reached the yards. Should be easy. We began the fun job of shifting portable yards, hauling heavy panels into place and prepping ourselves for a few days' camping and cattle work.

We waited until almost mid-morning to head out to the furthest windmill we would pick cattle up from, allowing them time to come in for a drink. The water point was about twenty kilometres from our planned yard-up point. Mum was in the buggy I often used for doing easy jobs with the dogs and I went on ahead on my quad bike. I had four dogs with me, including Cruise, while Mum had the rest of the team secured in the buggy ready to provide backup. Unfortunately, when

I idled the last few hundred metres down the road towards the mill, a small mob of cattle which had been grazing nearby startled and took off at a gallop, racing for the water point with no intention of stopping when they got there.

That's when I noticed we had a few unanticipated guests in the form of scrub bulls, spay cows and bullocks. Anyone who has spent time with pastoral stock will know these types of cattle are some of the hardest to handle, especially if they have experience at avoiding capture. Usually around here, if a steer has made it to bullock status, it's because he has mastered the art of hiding from the helicopter or giving the ground crew the slip through deeply ingrained cunning. Spay cows, on the other hand, have usually been culled for one or more of three main reasons: age, conformation or temperament. If she is still running loose a few years on, rest assured, it's not because she is lacking brains or bluster, and her previous temperament issue won't have mellowed with age.

Feeling fat and frisky due to the feed they had open access to, they looked like they weren't planning to wait around for the rest of my crew to arrive. Difficult cattle were not something I was prepared for. Even educated cattle can take some settling down when they are in good condition and 'fresh', but with these uneducated cattle outnumbering our few breeders, things soon went south.

And so our day began, with the mob of cattle bouncing between the dogs and me on the bike like ping-pong balls as we tried to settle them down and hold them on the water until Mum arrived with the rest of the team. The dogs put up a valiant effort, turning the cattle back time and time again, covering more ground to get in front of the cattle each time they dispersed. But we were just missing those extra legs that might have been enough to give us the upper hand. By the time Mum arrived on the scene with the buggy, we had a quarter of the number we had started with, the dogs were spent and my good spirits were in short supply.

There are some moments in life when maybe the best course of action is to quit while you are ahead or, as in this case, a little behind. In hindsight, this was one of those moments. But considering the effort spent so far, we decided to continue on with the cattle that hadn't scarpered yet. Have I mentioned I can be stubborn? I was working on the theory that the troublemakers had already left so the rest should be easy. Wrong theory.

We spent another hour untangling what felt like half a fence line, which Mum had collected from underneath the buggy, then picked up our now compliant but significantly smaller mob and headed off towards the next mill. It took a lot longer than I had anticipated. We lost time navigating through steep creeks that the cattle stubbornly insisted on following and we staggered into the next water point hours later with the quad bike running a bit worse for wear. Slight understatement really; it was doing its best to die and I was doing my best not to let it stall and shut down completely.

After the dogs all had a drink and a swim at the trough, we moved on again with fresh cattle joining us, which fortunately seemed inclined to behave. It was an hour or so later that things came to a head. Mum had doubled back while the cattle were walking well to look for my multi-tool pocketknife, lost during an impromptu bike-repair session. A new scrub bull chose this moment, while our crew was halved, to waltz into the mob with his scraggly followers, greet all the ladies and waltz back out again. With Mum out of radio reach and cattle splitting into two widespread mobs, I started asking too much of the dogs, who had already put in a good day's work, as we tried to hold things together. Eventually, I admitted defeat and stopped for the dogs to have a rest and a cool drink. It was then I realised I was missing one: Cruise.

Cruise had come to me as a ten-week-old pup from Queensland, full of self-confidence and, as he got older, an obsession with biting heels. There was very little about his work that I'd liked when he'd first started showing interest in stock but there was something in his nature that drew me to him. Little did I know that he would become one of my most talented and dedicated workers in the years to come, even losing the heel bite. The bond that was so persistent as a pup would grow as strong as any I have known with my dogs.

I knew the three most likely explanations for Cruise's absence: he'd got lost, injured or overheated. I was certain he must've got lost or, worst case, injured. It had been a long day, but we had been at the trough only an hour before, it was the middle of winter, although quite warm, we were in timbered country with access to shade, and Cruise had the best stamina of all my dogs, who were all tired but fine.

It took three hours and many miles tracking back over where I had ridden, covering everywhere I thought he might be. I didn't want him staying out overnight if he was lost, in case a pack of dingoes found him. I decided to make a last run along the creek line with the bike before I headed back to the stock camp to pick up my ute and return to camp out in the area that I thought Cruise might be in.

Suddenly I chanced across his prone form. I honestly thought he was already dead. He was unresponsive, his dry tongue hanging out of his mouth, his eyes squeezed tightly shut. But he was still breathing. Grasping on to that small glimmer of hope, I bathed his mouth with water and lifted his limp body onto the back of my quad bike, chanting his name and telling him it would be okay. Just keep breathing.

The next four days were some of the longest of my life. It took another six hours to get Cruise to the nearest vet, stopping at our homestead only long enough to call Del and ask if there was anything I could do for him before driving into town. Her advice: 'Just hurry.' We had nearly reached the highway when the first of the stomach cramps started. I doubled back towards the turnoff to the neighbours' homestead that I had flown past not long before, fearing that I'd run out of time.

Once again I called Del and asked her one of the hardest questions I've ever had to: 'I need to know if this is it, or is there still a chance. Once I leave here, I can't help him if it gets worse.'

I am thankful every day for her words, knowing the weight of what I was asking her. She couldn't see him, couldn't check him over herself, had nothing to go on but my desperate observations. 'If he is still there, if you can see he is conscious and the life is in his eyes … keep going.' So I did.

We arrived at the vet's at 10 pm, just as Cruise's intermittent stomach cramps became unrelenting. The vet was ready for us but I didn't need to see her face to know the prognosis wasn't good. We spent the night monitoring his vitals and trying to get his pain under control. We did everything we could with what we had available to stabilise him. Being a small country vet practice, and treating on a weekend to boot, supplies were limited. With every comprehensive blood test we took to check his vitals, I braced myself for the worst. We had agreed that if his kidneys started to fail, it would be kinder to let him go.

But Cruise surprised us both and he stayed strong. As long as there was a chance he could still recover and have a comfortable life, I was going to fight alongside him. So we fought. And we won. Four days later, we headed home, both mentally, physically and emotionally wrung out.

*

Impulse had come along for the ride to the vet, my consolation and company for the return trip if things didn't work out. He provided comfort and normality outside the clinic when I wasn't keeping vigil. Unlike Cruise and me, Impulse had a lovely holiday, spoilt by the vets and nurses alike. When it came time to head home, the traitor even hid under the vet nurse's desk, much to my chagrin and the clinic's amusement.

The incident with Cruise brought home to me just how easily overheating can occur. Overheating is a very common and dangerous threat to dogs across Australia. I'd been extremely aware of this danger, working and living in such a hot part of the country. But it seems, not careful enough. I'd grown complacent in the relative coolness of winter.

What we discovered during our time at the vet's was that at some stage in the long day mustering, Cruise had eaten a large amount of dried grass. This had exacerbated his dehydration and potentially limited his ability to rehydrate when he had access to water. Maybe it wasn't the main issue but it was definitely a contributing factor. Looking back, I can see the signs that he'd been in trouble, that something hadn't been right. I didn't recognise the severity of the situation when I should have, didn't appreciate that even in those Pilbara winter conditions, overheating was a very real threat.

The incident with Cruise taught me a very hard lesson about being prepared with electrolytes, shade and keeping better track of my dogs' whereabouts. Dogs can't sweat; they rely on releasing heat through panting, which exacerbates the dehydration that goes hand in hand with overheating. Having access to water and shade to cool down, electrolytes to replenish their mineral supply, and a chance for a rest through big jobs can be the difference between a successful day and a painful one. It's a lesson I don't wish to learn twice.

What haunts me now and will for years to come is the memory of Cruise trying to hop on the bike, of me reaching down to help him but not being strong enough to pull him up with one arm. Of making the decision not to stop, in case the bike stalled and this time didn't start again. Of telling him he'd just have to wait so I could stubbornly try once again to bend the cattle. He was asking for help and I didn't hear him. The place he asked for help is about where I found him, knocking on death's door hours later. And staring at his dusty, broken nail while he lay unconscious in the vet clinic, knowing he worked his heart out for me and was now paying the price, seared an image deep into my heart.

*

The continuing drought wasn't the only challenge we faced in 2020. During a routine shoulder operation, complications occurred that caused Dad to have a stroke, triggering seizures and a near complete loss of memory. It was a terrifying few weeks, watching as Dad slowly recovered, but the

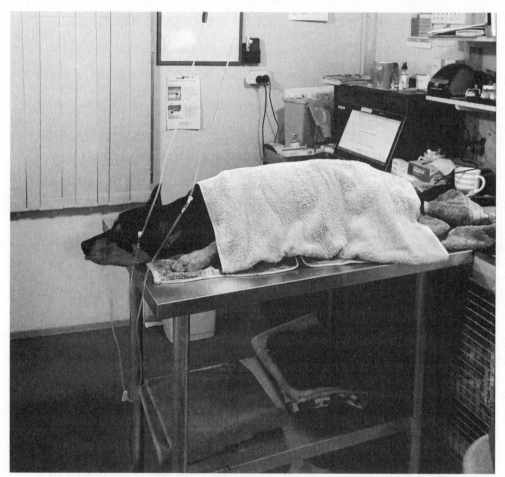

Cruise knocking on death's door.

consequences of that incident are still being felt. Apart from the ongoing medical issues, it was the temporary loss of his car and truck licence that really devastated Dad. He had been driving trucks since he was fourteen years old, built a business and life around them, so to lose his independence, even temporarily, was hard to endure. To suddenly have his legal right to drive the truck taken away from him was bad enough, but, once he had that back, to find his confidence and much of his mechanical knowledge had vanished was shattering. At 70 years old, to feel like you've lost five years of your life seemingly overnight, is no small thing. Adam and Murray stepped in to cover the trucking side of our business while Dad was 'out of action', fitting in trips between their own workloads as they could.

*

I was so sure winter would come through for us in 2020. Surely we had seen the worst of the drought already. But when we still hadn't received anything by mid-July, I realised we were looking down the barrel of another eight months before we could reasonably hope to have more feed on the ground. It was too long. We had made a promise to ourselves to never again reach the point we'd been at last year. We would see this drought out and use it as a chance to press the reset button. That was the light at the end of the tunnel that kept us going. This drought would end and, when it did, things were going to change; we were going to make sure we were never caught on the back foot again. Including the heifers we had brought home in anticipation of rain, we were only running at a quarter of our normal numbers, but it was still too many. After talking it over with Mum, and after a tearful phone call with Murray, the decision was made to fully destock the station of every animal we could get in. The relief, once the decision was made, was immediate. It was the right call for both our remaining cattle and our country

Something that gave us confidence in making these hard calls was the knowledge and decision-making tools we had learnt during Grazing for Profit courses both Murray and I had attended in early 2019.

In February that year, before we started mustering, I had flown to Kununurra to attend the course run by Resource Consulting Service (RCS). By that stage, I was firmly holding the reins of the station and more than ever felt there was still too much I didn't know. With a focus on regenerative agriculture, the course covered everything from accounts and budgeting to the life cycles of plants and management of livestock. It was an intense week but fantastic. I came out wishing I had completed it ten years earlier when Murray had done it, but better late than never, and perhaps I was actually at a point where I got more from the course than I would have done earlier. Murray completed the same course the following month at a venue closer to the farm, putting us both on the same page as we looked towards the year ahead.

There was one poignant message I heard during the course that echoed in my head for the next two years and beyond. The RCS presenter David McLean mentioned in passing that if you were checking the weather forecasts daily, you hadn't correctly matched your stocking rate to your grazing capacity. Basically, it was a pretty good indicator you had too many cattle. A few of us in the room had looked sheepishly at each other.

Until that point, I had always felt more interested in our cattle than the country that sustained them, apart from admiring the grass when it grew. But after the course in Kununurra, I looked at the country around me with new eyes. It was parched; the reduced water table and subsoil moisture were being felt by the trees, bushes and shrubs alike. Between our cattle and the excess feral donkeys that were competing with them, any grass that had grown last winter was long gone. We were in trouble.

Making the decision to fully destock was one thing; finding somewhere for the cattle to go was another entirely. Agistment was still hard to find as properties south of us in the Gascoyne region started feeling the pinch of drought too and were shifting cattle out of that area. A chance phone call to a local grazier was a turning point in the year for me. Evan and his wife, Robin, had already committed the bulk of their country to other properties that needed agistment, but they had some spare country available that could hold a few of our best breeders. These cows, along with our breeders still held on long-term agistment from the year before, would be our starting point when the time came again.

Evan and Robin have been practising regenerative management on their nearby station for the last twenty years. After destocking years earlier, they had travelled the same path that Murray and I were now embarking on. They had attended a Grazing for Profit course and given up traditional management methods in favour of cell grazing. Cell grazing is the practice of dividing larger paddocks up into small ones and moving cattle every few days or as the feed dictates, allowing for better utilisation of the feed available. A good method when managed right and a very unusual concept for our area. The results were easy to see. Supplementing their agistment income with contract machinery work and tourism, Evan and Robin were able to easily control the numbers of stock on their country each year, and the country looked fantastic for it. They weren't entirely safe from drought, though. Even with no grazing pressure, I could see when I visited the property the spinifex dying across the hills and trees curling up their roots. There is only so much the country can do without subsoil moisture, but the recovery on areas with retained ground cover would be swift with the first rains.

It was while I was visiting Evan and seeing where we could agist our stock that he mentioned they were struggling to find staff to help run the cells. I jumped at the chance. I had been hoping to see up close what Evan was doing with his grazing management. Very shortly we would have next to no cattle at home to look after, so this was too good an opportunity to pass up.

Over the next few months I bounced back and forth between home and Evan and Robin's Cheela Plains. It was a bit of a juggling act, working at one property while still overseeing the running of another, but fortunately Mum was keeping things ticking along well. There was so much for me, my dogs and the cattle to learn at Cheela, including educating new stock to hot wires and quick paddock moves. We got quite the education in electricity ourselves along the way. Impulse, one of my black-and-tan male kelpies, copped a good zap when his tail got too close to the hot wire while having a quick dip in the water trough between shifts, which I admittedly found quite hilarious until karma got me back with a hefty zap through faulty pliers not long after. I swear his smug expression said, 'Not so funny now, is it!'

*

Between my stints at Cheela Plains, I had to organise the mustering in of our remaining Glen Florrie cattle so our breeders could be moved across into their new paddock. Mum and I gathered the smaller mobs in on our own with a few panels to make a yard and the dogs to help us walk the cattle in from water points. We timed our big musters with the school holidays so we had plenty of help in the way of friends and family. When they took in the cattle they were helping us muster to send off on agistment, their comments of 'They look really good, I thought their condition would be poor!' gave me a quiet feeling of satisfaction.

'Yes, they do,' I replied. 'Last year we had poor cattle and poor country. This year we have healthy cattle and poor country. Next time we run into dry times, I hope we make decisions early when we still have healthy cattle and healthy country.'

It was during one of these holiday musters that Jonique, a Murdoch Veterinary student staying with us for a few weeks, rode her horse over to where I was following a couple of cows on the bike as we tailed the mob.

'Teesh, I think Cash might have an injury.'

I looked around for the dog in question.

'He was just here having a drink a minute ago, surely he can't have hurt himself already.'

Apparently he could. When he jumped up onto the bike at my whistle, I could see a large flap of skin peeled down on his shoulder and glistening a lovely bloody red.

'Oh jeez, Cash, how'd you manage that? We aren't even doing anything!'

I pulled out my makeshift medical kit and started applying a salt wash and bandage to his wound. Cash paid me no mind at all. I wasn't sure if it was adrenalin or a high pain threshold but I was grateful for the calmness, though it really made no difference to my dismal bandaging attempt.

Reluctantly resigned to riding on the bike for the rest of the afternoon, Cash somehow retained his noble bearing, despite looking like I'd wrapped a nappy around his chest. It was our last day out at stock camp before we headed back to the homestead that evening. After another rinse of his war wound and a better attempt at a bandage, Cash headed off with Mum while I drove the stock truck loaded with cattle. My intention was for Cash to get back to the house a bit sooner than I did so my Aunty Jan, Mum's younger sister and a nurse, could attend to his wound with the help of Jonique and the other Vet students.

I was nearly finished unloading the cattle back at the homestead yards when Mum arrived out of the dark. 'We need you to come and help us with Cash. He's stressed and won't settle. They think he needs you.'

'I highly doubt I'll make much difference but okay, I'll be there in a sec.'

I closed up the gates then headed back to the house, where I sat down on the floor next to the patient. 'Hey, Cash dog, what's going on?'

Cash whined quietly, nuzzled his nose into my hand then calmly lay down next to me. I heard the 'Aww's coming from Cash's makeshift medical team around me and looked up.

'He wouldn't do that before, he wasn't like this at all!'

My heart melted. 'Oh, Cash, the secret is out now. You big softie!'

Cash proceeded to be the perfect patient as we cleaned and doctored his wound. Any adrenalin had long since worn off and it was sheer bravery and the incredible pain tolerance of these beautiful dogs that held him still and unflinching. In a bid to keep the staples and his torn skin in place, we dressed Cash in one of my long-sleeved shirts, which covered the wound well. It was sheer fluke the shirt was covered in love hearts. Cash was not impressed.

Over the course of the next week, Cash would tolerate our ministrations. He would stand tall and still while we doctored him, only objecting if we tried actually holding him in place, a practice we soon realised was unnecessary and quickly abandoned. He didn't mind the house privileges but would have been back at work in a heartbeat if I'd let him.

This was my first hint that I had a very accident-prone dog on my hands. Since then, Cash's injuries have been inventive but luckily none too serious. He's lost a canine tooth and cut a main vein low on his foot. My first inkling something was amiss was a pretty impressive blood trail he left me to follow,

Cash tolerating our medical intervention on his shoulder.

but then he couldn't understand what all the fuss was about. I think he just likes the sooking.

Cash had only been with me for around five months when he injured his shoulder. He is full brother to my main bitch, Diamond, and I originally only had him on loan as a sire with the option to buy. Two weeks into that loan I decided he was too good to lose and Cash officially joined my team. He had passed through a few hands before he came into my camp and it showed a bit in his attitude. He was initially a hard nut to crack, a very self-assured male with little need for affection. But I started getting glimpses of his softer side and I loved seeing that come through. Without a doubt, we butt heads more than any others in my team. He has an exceptionally strong work drive, which can lead to some temporary or not so temporary deafness if he feels a job isn't done.

He is also a spruiker. He loves to stir up the other males in my team with his cockiness. He has a wicked bite that you can see coming from a mile off as he hurls himself through the air at whichever unlucky beast pushed a nose out too far. Only half the time is the bite warranted.

But his cover is beautiful, his desire to work second to none. He'll cast out wide in search of livestock and has little need for commands, not that he listens anyway. He is a proven sire, throwing great pups to a number of different bitches. And deep down, he is an affectionate boy. He huffs a little to gain your attention and will sit on your foot with his back to you once he's got it. If I'm away for a while, he jumps up with his back against me, whining until I give him a hug. I have to double lock his kennel or he'll squeeze out an impossibly small gap and arrive back at the house almost before I do. His tail wags up and down, a quirk that is quite hereditary it turns out. A beautiful, strong and competent character, I wouldn't be without him now.

Chapter Sixteen

Gossip Girl

**'Everyone thinks they have the best dog,
and none of them are wrong.'**
– Anonymous

It was a few weeks after I started working at Cheela Plains that Miss Gossip Girl came barking into my life.

I was first approached by a producer to participate in the *Muster Dogs* documentary in early 2019, at the suggestion of Neil McDonald. Though I appreciated being considered, the timing wasn't great. We were coping with the ravages of drought and the property was looking parched. It wasn't something I felt I could commit to. But in 2020, one of the producers got back in touch. The documentary had been shelved temporarily the year before but now everything was lining up and they still wanted me to be a part of it.

The show planned to take five well-bred young pups, all from the same litter, and place them in working homes across Australia. From a cattle trainer working across stations in the far north to a sheep farmer in the south of Australia, every home was unique. Each participant who took a pup would have the chance to highlight the role working dogs played in their life and business, as they spent the next twelve months fitting the new pup into their team.

What intrigued me about the project, was the goal of showcasing the importance of working dogs across Australia. Before having my own team, I had no idea of how truly valuable good dogs could be. So the opportunity to highlight this and encourage others to consider utilising working dogs was tempting.

Another attraction of the show was the incredibly talented and well-known dog trainers involved. Neil McDonald and his equally talented wife, Helen, would set the 'milestone markers' that each participant and their pups were encouraged to reach by certain ages. These assessments would be filmed to track the development of the pups. At one time or another, all of us involved in the documentary have attended one or more of Neil's schools so we knew what we were in for.

Peter Barr, who I had met on my earlier trips east, provided another perspective, with his experience in dog training. And the other big name involved in the show was Joe Spicer from GoGetta Kelpie stud. Joe has developed a reputation as a reliable breeder of working kelpies and this has not come about by fluke. He is very knowledgeable about the different bloodlines, and over the years has been very selective in his breeding of working dogs. His dogs are in strong demand in working homes across Australia, as well as on the trialling ground where Joe holds the title of winning four Australian Yard Dog Trial Championships. Considering that the grandsire of these pups, GoGetta Brue, is a twice Australian Yard Dog Champion himself, they have a pretty impressive pedigree backing them up.

I had been wanting to get a pup from Joe for quite a while now, to see if it would suit my station work. Seems like I was about to have my chance.

The other four participants I either knew by name or had already met. Rob Tuncks was the only sheep farmer amongst us and he had his little red-and-tan kelpie pup specially delivered to his farm in South Australia by Joe Spicer himself.

Rob and Lucifer's early days together were a little rocky. Rob's intention was for his new pup to be a well-socialised inside working pet, but after Lucifer's first night in the laundry resulted in a chewed-up door, the pup's original name of Zap was promptly dropped in favour of the more apt Lucifer. Guess Lucifer wasn't a fan of special pampering.

Annie is a beautiful black-and-tan bitch pup who firmly nestled herself into the affections of her owner, Frank Finger.

Frank lives in the central highlands in Queensland, just outside of Clermont, where he and his family run three cattle properties. Annie, aka the Princess, gets her own special supply of treats, specifically honey-and-soy rice crackers. The only ones she likes, apparently. 'I think at my age now, nearly 70, I can afford to spoil one. I've never spoilt a dog before,' Frank said in defence.

Also meeting her new owner, CJ Scotney, at Clermont was Spice, a gorgeous red-and-tan girl whose bustling energy was immediately evident. CJ and her family had travelled from their cattle property in the Northern Territory to attend one of Neil's schools, hosted, as many had been over the last 24 years, by Frank. Apparently the two young pups immediately showed the difference in their personalities, with Annie lying docile in Frank's arms, and Spice doing everything but that. CJ wondered what she was in for.

Joni Hall was another participant. She had met her inscrutable red-and-tan pup, Chet, when he arrived in Fitzroy Crossing in northern Western Australia. Educating cattle across a number of stations in the Northern Territory and the top of Western Australia and Queensland, Joni handles an incredible number of stock each year with her team of kelpies and is known for being a straight shooter. 'The hardest part will be keeping him alive,' said Joni. 'He just doesn't really think things through yet.'

Then there was my new little charge.

If you've ever had a kelpie, you would know that it's true when I say, they are often too smart for our own good. The pup I received from Joe Spicer, Gossip Girl, is the perfect example of this. She is a dog who is almost human, her sharp mind often keeping me on my toes. She was the last pup to be dropped off by Chet, the pet transport operator who delivered Gossip and her siblings all the way from Victoria and inspired the name of Joni's pup. Meeting me in Karratha, he handed over a noisy, wriggling black-and-tan bundle of energy. With an impossibly cute, almost gremlin-looking face framing lively brown eyes, I knew we were in for some fun times.

Our first days were interesting, to say the least. I was spending the majority of my time working at Cheela Plains Station and now I had a feisty little ten-week-old pup underfoot as well. Leaving her behind when I headed out at 6.30am wasn't really an option. She acquired her name Gossip Girl with good reason. She had a lot to say for herself and wasn't shy about saying it. Loudly. Come to think of it, she still isn't. Her early-morning vocals weren't something I was game to inflict on my sleeping neighbours, who happened to be the resident chefs, and I was sincerely hoping they would continue to feed me.

Some weeks later I sent Joe a message with a few photos of her early adventures and a cheeky comment about the reason for her name.

His reply: 'Good! Taught her well, she's demanding your attention!'

Well, she sure got that.

*

The first task for Gossip and me was learning how to ride a two-wheel motorbike together. After a few false starts, we soon had it down pat, or at least we thought we did, and I decided it was time to pull out the GoPro. We had been supplied with a GoPro to get some footage for the documentary, and here's a tip: don't get cocky too soon. And for the love of dogs, don't video it if you do.

After I fitted the GoPro to the front handlebars of the bike, carefully positioned so that it captured Gossip's proud profile, we headed off into the paddock to check stock. This was a track I took at least four times a day, so I knew which gates I had left open. Gates in this scenario are often a single wire in the fence pulled down to the ground and held there by a truck tyre on top. A great system that had proven a very effective time-saver when passing through empty paddocks regularly. But, as we found out, it wasn't foolproof.

What I didn't realise (and you can see where this is going, can't you?) is that the previous night when I had come home on this track in the Toyota ute, the wire had come out from under the tyre and flicked up behind us. So as Gossip and

I jauntily cruised down the airstrip and around the corner into the next paddock, we weren't expecting a wire to be strung up barely a metre in front of us. Instinct had me grabbing the brakes and clutch as I watched in bemused horror as my little passenger did a very graceful cartwheel over the handlebars into the soft bull dust beyond.

And so our movie career together began ...

It seems to me, as soon as you press record on a video camera, things start going awry. Shifting a mob of cattle between paddocks with a few of my older dogs on the ground and Gossip riding shotgun seemed like a good chance to get some footage. To set the scene, I asked Adam, who was staying with us for a few days while on a break from work, to start filming with the GoPro while I got Gossip settled on the bike with me. For whatever reason (I blame the camera), that day we both managed to make a simple everyday task unbelievably awkward. Gossip's foot braced against my face while my arm was hooked uncomfortably around her neck. Hiding his laughter well, Adam kindly shifted the focus of the camera out onto the cattle while we righted ourselves and pretended nothing amiss had happened.

In the end, all of our early GoPro footage was lost and, as devastating as it was to lose so many of Gossip's early adventures, there was a small part of me quietly thankful that some of our gaffes would never see the light of day.

My little offsider Gossip Girl 'helping' me at Cheela Plains Station.

*

As the days passed, Gossip and I spent countless hours together, shifting cattle around the cells on Cheela Plains, heading out on the motorbike, searching for waterholes and checking for stray cattle tracks. She would ride up front while we shifted stock between paddocks and checked fences for electrical faults. I soon learnt the value of the three-metre drag rope Neil had instructed us to attach permanently to the pups. Gossip reached the stage all pups seem to go through of not coming when she was called. Brave enough to hop off the bike if I did, she was too small to hop back on and ratbag enough to be disinclined to try; she was still too young to run behind the bike but fast enough to easily evade my capture. It was not a fun combination. Easily fixed if I remembered to clip her drag rope on, which I most often did not. In this case I was the one in need of training.

We also spent many enjoyable hours travelling in the ute between mobs of cattle. Early on, only the driver's side air-conditioning worked with any efficiency but, still, Gossip was content to lie beside me with her head jammed between the seats. To this day, this is her preferred position if she rides in the front. Though she really is too big now for pup privileges and should graduate to riding on the back with the big dogs full-time, sometimes she still gets to ride shotgun with me.

Gossip had two favourite tricks she liked to play on me during our drives. Her favourite seemed to be waiting until the aircon had finally started to take the edge off our lovely Pilbara spring temperatures of low 40 degrees before gassing me out and requiring my window to be wound down in a hurry. She'd raise her head as I gasped her name with my nose out the window and look at me with an expression that plainly said, 'What's your issue?'

The other trick pups seem to have innate knowledge of is locking doors and Gossip was no exception. Second nature to me now is winding down the window an arm's width each time I step out of the vehicle. The number of times I have returned to my driver's door to find the lock down and Gossip's wide-eyed innocent face peering back at me is uncountable. So is the number of times I have had to make the mad dash around to the passenger side hoping I can open that door before it too has the lock stepped on. To add injury to insult, sometimes Gossip would wait until I was just reaching the bonnet before she'd stand on the car horn and cause my heart rate to spike to triple time, grinning at me over the steering wheel as I tried to recover from the heart attack.

*

'Teesh, I've lost Cruise ...'

These were the last words I expected to hear when I answered the call from a private number at seven o'clock one night while working at Cheela Plains. But as soon as I heard the delay indicating the call was from our station satellite phone, my breath caught in my throat and a million different scenarios started running through my head, none of them good.

'I'm so sorry, Teesh,' Mum kept repeating, over and over again.

'Wait, slow down, breathe ... what do you mean, lost? As in missing or ...?' I paused, wrapping my towel around me tighter as I abandoned my shower and frantically searched for better phone reception to keep the connection.

'He's fallen off the ute and I can't find him. I've been back over my tracks and it looks like he fell off near Stockroute Well but there's no sign of him.' Mum was crying now, the stress of the last six hours of searching finally breaking through.

'Okay, he's alive, then, thank god, just lost. We can work with that. It's okay, Mum, calm down. We'll find him. I'm heading home, I'll be there as soon as I can.'

Four hours later, after playing over and over in my head every possible scenario I could conjure up, I arrived home to be met at the gate by none other than the dog of the hour himself. The one Mum was still out searching for, leaving dishes of water and old clothing with my scent on them along the road she had been travelling when she lost him. It seems Cruise had headed cross country, avoiding all tracks that might have let us see his footprints, to meet me on the homestead lawn upon my arrival late that night. To say his and Mum's reunion was a teary one would be an understatement, and I was left wondering why we put ourselves through this stress time and time again.

Cruise's adventure into the night, 30 kilometres from home, was my fault. I didn't have an easy set-up on the ute for Mum to use to secure the dogs when she did a mill run. Working away, I was asking my family to care for the dogs and it was on me to have had things arranged conveniently for them. We found Cruise or, I should say, he found his way home with no help from us, but we got lucky. He had beaten the odds by avoiding injury, maintaining his sense of direction without the use of roads, and not straying into the neighbouring country which was heavily baited for wild dogs; all of this in the heat of summer, through a 45-degree day, without access to any water.

On top of this, Cruise wasn't 100 per cent back to his beautiful self, mentally or physically, after his overheating episode a few months earlier.

After the number of hours spent searching, the sleepless nights driving around, the worry, stress and panic I have felt over the years when dogs have been lost off vehicles, I should have learnt well before now the shortcut just isn't worth the few minutes gained. It doesn't take long to organise a short chain or rope to safely secure the dogs onto the back of the vehicle under shade while doing mill runs around the station. It's worth every second for the peace of mind it provides and the heartache it can save. For us and the dogs.

*

Due to our previous filming experiences, I was pretty nervous when the time came for a real film crew to show up at home for Gossip's four-month 'assessment'. This involved demonstrating a few things Neil and Helen had advised the pups should be showing by this age, including knowing their name, dragging a rope without being fazed by it and, if possible, showing some early pup-appropriate instinct about stock. With my other dogs, this would have been a pretty easy ask, but with Gossip, I was having a few doubts.

Although we had spent so much time together while working at Cheela Plains, I felt like we had a very tenuous bond. Gossip had a self-assured take-no-prisoners attitude that reminded me of Diamond. She had captivated me from day one, though I often felt like I was trying to tame a wildcat that couldn't care less about getting my attention.

In the week before the film crew arrived I sensed a subtle shift in our relationship. Gossip seemed to come more easily when I called and was more responsive and keen to please. And on that hot day of filming, she did an amazing job. She tirelessly followed me around and came each time when I called, take after take, until it was captured from all angles.

Every time we asked her again to walk across the lawn with no lead to show off our 'Bluetooth connection', as Neil likes to call it, I was secretly thinking, please don't disconnect! But she held in there, even as the heat crept up and the shade looked so tempting for a camp.

We attempted to recreate the scene where she drank out of my hat, which I had captured in a photo a few months earlier, after one particularly long, hot bike ride out to find a dried-up waterhole. Gossip kindly accommodated us and took a few laps from the hat, though I'm sure she was wondering why the perfectly good water bowl nearby wasn't sufficient. For such a young pup, she was amazingly tolerant.

To show her early working instinct, we had no access to suitable stock other than the large poddy weaners we had held only for the maremmas, and the chooks. Neither is an ideal animal to have such a young pup out with but the task was set so we gave it a go. The chooks worked okay, she stalked them like a pro and, many months on, she still does. If you want a dog that doesn't harass chooks, my best advice is: keep it away from the chooks while it's a pup.

We also got lucky with the poddies. Gossip moved them around and managed to dodge any knocks, doing enough for the documentary before I tucked her back out of harm's way, and heaved a sigh of relief that we all came away intact, especially her confidence. Sometimes one well-placed kick is all it takes to set a young pup back, sometimes permanently.

*

'Whatever you do, don't come back in January!' My parting words after the fairly scorching November shoot must've been ringing in cameraman Greg's ears when he showed up again to film our six-month assessment in … January. As it turned out, the three days the film crew were here happened to be our hottest days of the whole summer, hitting 52 degrees Celsius in the shade of the verandah. It was brutal.

This time the assessment involved showing that our pups could jump up on a motorbike (nailed it), walk alongside with no lead (no problem), show basic herding instincts (easy-peasy) and be able to demonstrate one of my least favourite of Neil's training steps, the quarter bubble. This is where our wheels fell off.

The quarter bubble is an exercise Neil McDonald designed to teach pups to move smoothly around stock, and to teach the livestock how to be a trainer mob, which requires a fair degree of tolerance and trust. Gossip and I finally had suitable stock to practise this on, in the form of five boar goats which would be our trainer mob.

We practised our balancing (where Gossip would draw the stock towards me, the first instinct we encourage in the pups) and the quarter bubble in preparation for the assessment, but it is a fact of life that I suck at this exercise. Truly, I make it look so much harder than it should be. Gossip's penchant for working in close on her stock did not do me any favours either. Not necessarily a bad thing, it just meant I had less time to get into the right position to guide her around the trainers before she would end up in too close to them. A habit that a few of her siblings were also starting to show.

But we did our demonstration for the assessment and bumbled our way through it. Just don't expect to see any grand display of perfect bubble techniques from Gossip and me if you watch the documentary!

*

'We'll set up here to get the shot of the poddy calves walking out with the maremmas.'

The gear was being carefully readied to recreate a scene we had started to capture the day before but missed due to technical issues. Of course, the lighting, the cattle and Ringer had all operated perfectly like they had read a script. I had my doubts it would go that smoothly twice.

The camera was only a few feet away from the route that our poddy calves would surely be taking as they headed back out into the paddock. 'Yep, that will be the perfect spot. The issue is going to be their walking into the camera rather than past it!' I said.

Sure enough, the calves wandered out like they had been trained for it until they got within a few feet of the camera. Then they crowded around with noses outstretched and tongues at the ready, looking to chew on the gear I don't want to even imagine the price of. They were oblivious to the many attempts to shuffle them on as the camera tried in vain to capture the maremmas strolling past behind them.

The perks of turning hand-raised calves into a trainer mob are that they are extremely quiet and unfazed by most new situations. The drawbacks are they are extremely quiet and super curious about most new situations, like cameras, unfamiliar cars and new people to hit up for a scratch. Poddies take the old saying 'Never work with young kids and animals' to a whole new level, as the beleaguered film crew were quickly finding out.

After the last morning of filming, we waved the crew off and Mum, Adam and I conceded the heat truly was unbearable. We headed down to our local swimming hole to spend the rest of the afternoon lounging around the cool spring with the dogs, enjoying the shade of the paperbarks. There's got to be some perks to a Pilbara summer.

*

Unfortunately, our goats didn't stay with us for long. As the wet season began and some beautiful rain passed through, we had an outbreak of stable flies. Some trigger in the season must've provided the perfect storm for them and they hatched in unbelievable numbers in the hay around our cattle yards. That just so happened to be where our goats were housed.

Taking pity on them, I shifted them down to the poddy pens we had set up behind the house near the river. They were soon spending their afternoons grazing the shrubs and lawn around the homestead yard, happy as can be. Not so Angel. She took exception to the interlopers in 'her' yard and would chase them back into their pen if she caught them wandering. After a couple of days, she would have settled down but before that happened, they took matters into their own hands.

Choosing the one night I was left in charge, they found a gap in the gate and disappeared down the house creek. With the recent rains leaving the rivers resembling mini-oases full of green grass and trickling streams, not even the promise of pellets could lure them home. Despite our best efforts over the next week and many hours spent trying to track them, we never came across more than their tracks. I haven't entirely given up hope of stumbling across them on some obscure part of the property, but, realistically, I think the dingoes will beat me to it.

Chapter Seventeen

Muster Dogs

'If you've got grass, you've got options.'

— My mantra through the drought

Mum, Adam and I sat on the edge of a rocky outcrop, watching the swirling ochre-red water pass by with a muted roar as the dogs explored around behind us. The date palms scattered behind our house, which had survived the drought, stood strong against the flow, as their dry fronds and perished comrades disappeared downstream. The air hung heavy with moisture, fragrant with the scents of soil and plant life. We were sitting at a junction of two river systems and the resulting flow of water was impressive. Even after living on Glen Florrie for 27 years, witnessing the full power of the water in flow was still as awe-inspiring as ever.

In the early days of 2021, we received our first decent summer rainfall in four years. It was kind, gentle rain, delivering a beautiful 120 millimetres over five days in a steady soaking fall. With the ground so parched and bare, our infiltration rates were reduced, and we lost what couldn't be immediately absorbed as it drained into the river systems. But that's part of the cycle too. Our underground streams would be replenished, along with the waterholes that had disappeared in the early days of the drought.

I thought with the first rains, I would be overcome with a sweeping feeling of relief, but it didn't happen. I think I was too scared to believe the drought was finally over; that there wasn't more disappointment waiting just around the corner to steal the joy away. In any case, we still needed follow-up rain. As good as this start was, the grass shoots would need continuing drinks to keep them going long enough to get properly established again. Much of our feed base had died, the old buffel-grass clumps blackened and unresponsive. But even in death, they offered support to life. New germination would emerge from seeds trapped in their remains and the withered root system would allow water to seep underground.

It wasn't until we started to see evidence of the country responding to the life-sustaining rain that some of the weight of the last four years started to lift. Maybe we were finally on the other side. The country could start to recover and we could press the reset button we had been promising to do if we could just hold on and make it through the drought – mentally, physically and financially. After so long in 'disaster management', we could finally start controlling our direction. Our common goal was to do everything we could to protect our country, our family and our business from experiencing anything like it again. Murray and I had the desire for change, appreciation for the education it would require and the motivation to make it happen.

It wasn't just the station that needed this rain. The southern farms had suffered as well, carrying too much of the load while they were also experiencing dry seasons. Even with the plans Murray had in place for repairing and regenerating the sandy soil, the toll of the previous overstocking with cattle from the station would be felt for a while to come.

One of the biggest take-homes for me from the drought was understanding that the earlier we made decisions, the more options we had. Once we decided to destock, I went from checking the weather charts umpteen times a day to barely at all. It finally didn't feel like we were on tenterhooks waiting for the rain to come anymore. Obviously we were still hoping it would, but the lives of our poorly conditioned stock weren't at stake if it didn't. We were prepared either way. We knew what cattle we had left were on good feed on agistment and if worse came to worst, we could sell them too and start again from scratch when things turned around. Our priorities were able to shift from the management of our cattle to the management of our country, and working at Cheela Plains gave me a chance to see in practice the feed-budgeting and grazing-management principles I had learnt at the RCS course two years earlier.

When the rains did finally start falling, we didn't rush to bring our cattle home. We held the majority of them on agistment and lease for as long as we could to give our country a chance to recover. We had asked too much of the land over the last few years and it was time to pay some of that 'capital debt' back. Hopefully, as time goes on and with new grazing strategies and management practices in place, we can build more resilience into both our business and our landscape. The same resilience my dogs show ever day as they step up as key players in the future of our property.

*

Gossip Girl's nine-month assessment was, to understate it a little, hectic. Throughout the documentary, the effects of the drought had been on full display with our ravaged landscape and empty cattle yards telling the story. Finally, now, a few months after our welcome rain in early January, we could start to show the other side of the dry. The country was a patchwork quilt of different shades of green as new grasses shot up, trees and shrubs became covered in new growth, and the rain washed off their dusty coats. It was a soothing balm for the soul, watching the landscape spring back to life, with birds and insects enlivening our morning and evening walks with the dogs. With the growing season coming to a halt down south where some of our cattle remained on agistment, it was also time to bring the first of our girls home.

One of the producers of *Muster Dogs* was adamant she wanted the film crew to capture this moment: when the trucks travelled down our long driveway and unloaded the cattle back into the yards they had been shifted from two years earlier, with no idea of when or even if they would come back. It was the start of a new chapter and I understood why she wanted to catch it on film. But it was going to be a busy week receiving the cattle, processing them out into the paddocks and filming Gossip in between. I'd just plan carefully, no worries.

Mum was away for a few weeks over this period but Adam and I could cover things. We were also providing meals and accommodation to a mining company while they did some drilling, but they were scheduled to be gone the week before the cattle arrived. Worst case scenario, we had some breathing space before the film crew and cattle trucks would arrive, and surely the drilling crew's ten-day program wouldn't be extended by a full week. Surely?

As if Mother Nature was enjoying an inside joke with herself, the week we booked the trucks to shift the cattle home, she sent in a storm to make the driveway impassable. Not that we were complaining. The best reason for changing plans is rain. And I was secretly relieved for other reasons. If ever there was an unlucky drilling company, it was the one staying with us. They had breakdown after breakdown, and each day a new unexpected issue arose that stalled their work. Fortunately the rain's delay for the trucks and the film crew getting in would give us time for the drilling to be wrapped up and I wouldn't be catering for eight drillers on top of everything else.

Well, did Mother Nature laugh. The ten-day drilling program ran a month over schedule, so with the truckies plus the film crew, I was catering for fifteen people and managing cattle when the time came for Gossip Girl's nine-month assessment. And we only had two and a half days to capture everything they needed on film, in between the cattle work. It wasn't what I would call a fun time, at least for me. Gossip had a ball.

The film crew turned up the night before the trucks and cattle were due to arrive. I had asked Dad to give me a call from the highway before he lost phone reception and we would meet him out near Danger Bend, where the road cuts through the hills. This had been identified as a scenic spot where the team could film the trucks returning with the cattle with a drone. We headed out to wait for Dad there and captured the cover shot for this book while we waited. Once Dad was in radio range, I met him down the road and passed on the plans for the sequence. The drone was going to fly along just in front of the truck before filming him curving around the corner and beyond. Easy enough.

As we waited back up the road for Dad to crest the hill with the drone at the ready, Greg, the same unlucky cameraman who was involved in our previous two filming segments, started looking a bit nervous. 'He's going too fast!' he exclaimed as we watched the prime mover with its five decks of cattle pass by in a cloud of dust with the drone desperately trying to keep up.

'Okay, I'll ask Charlie to take it a bit slower,' I said, as I called up Charlie, the second truck driver, on the radio. Unfortunately, Charlie hadn't been on our road before and I didn't explain the terrain very well. Though it looked picture perfect from where we were filming, Charlie later told me we were close to filming his truck stuck on the hill, rather than cresting over it.

After a few more stops to jump ahead of the trucks and film them crossing rivers or travelling along open flats (where the wind changed direction and Charlie ended up disappearing in Dad's dust – less than ideal), they were finally pulling up at the unloading ramp and our tired girls could rest their weary legs.

It was bitter-sweet, watching our cattle being unloaded back into my care. Cows that had fallen pregnant despite the trying time, heifers that had been too good to let go of. These girls were our fresh start. But the past few years had shaken my confidence and left me feeling unprepared and unqualified to be in charge of these lives and this property again. When we made the hard decisions – to destock, to sell, to hold on, to let go – we had to have faith they were the right decisions at the time, the best we could do with the information we had on hand. But the fact remained, it was new ground for me and for all of us. Dad, in particular, really struggled with the concept of completely destocking, after his years in the industry and never making that call himself. We didn't know then if we would survive financially and, to be honest, we still don't. The repercussions of a drought are felt for years after the rains return. We might have turned the corner, but it wasn't smooth running from here. Having breeder cows back on the property was definitely a good start, but it would be two years before their progeny would provide an income. In the meantime, the bills don't stop coming and we still have a property to maintain and look after.

These were some of the thoughts running through my head as I watched the trailers slowly empty the cattle. Gratitude and apprehension in equal measures. Most farmers don't have a film crew on the ground recording these critical occasions. I don't recall what I said in my interview; I only know

I struggled to put everything I was feeling in that moment into the right words.

*

Gossip Girl and I started on the back foot with the assessment ... and stayed there. Though we had the poddies, they were almost too dog-educated for what Gossip needed now. We didn't have any suitable stock on hand to practise the tasks we'd been set until it was time to film them, so what was captured wasn't a polished performance. Far from it. We were asked to show our pups working the sides and pushing a mob along, demonstrating a 'stop and sit', and a basic cast. Yeah, well ...

With the film crew waiting nearby, we had spent the morning drafting the cattle, processing calves and pulling out a line of suitable weaners, which I briefly handled with my older dogs, before Gossip and I gave it a go solo. The weaners did well really, and Gossip, too, considering how little we had done leading up to this. But she was still enjoying biting heels, flanks, anywhere she could reach, which was not conducive to calm cattle. Still, we had ticked the first item off the list. Gossip's 'stop and sit' on stock was non-existent, but we played around a bit, getting her to stop next to me when I walked around the yards. I'm sure that's not what the task was really asking for, but I wasn't going to argue if it got me off the hook for more filming.

When it came time to demonstrate our cast, though, I had a feeling the wheels were about to fall off. Gossip's penchant for working close was not conducive to a natural cast and we hadn't had any opportunity to practise. I kept Impulse, one of my naturally wide-working older dogs, on hand to help draw Gossip around behind the stock, with limited success. It wasn't something we could practise and learn in the short time we had available but we had to fill the brief. We decided to try getting some footage with the drone outside the yards for a different scene.

'We've got limited goes at this,' I warned, as I let the weaners wander down the fence the requisite 50 metres. 'If it works, it'll be a fluke and we won't get it twice. So make sure you get it the first time, right?'

I set us up (not well enough, I should have had a rake in my hand as an arm extension to help me guide her) and sent Gossip and Impulse around the mob. It wasn't perfect, but Gossip didn't cut the mob in half, and as I shut the gates behind the weaners after yarding them again, I breathed out a sigh of relief. Thank god that was done. Then I heard Sally, the director, pipe up: 'Teesh, we need to do it again so we can film it from the ground.' My head dropped to the gate with a thunk.

The second time round was not a success. The weaners had become fed up with Gossip's wild bite and as she split the mob, one of our quiet poddy weaners finally decided enough was enough. He disappeared out the back of the mob with Gossip and Angel, the 'failed' maremma, in hot pursuit. Five minutes and one voice box later, he had disappeared through a fence and I was beyond mad, blistering the sound man's ears with my thoughts about the whole proceedings.

It wasn't just the stress of things going wrong on film – which I was starting to adamantly believe was an inevitable fact of life – that was getting to me. I was running short on sleep, the cooking was a full-time job on its own, we had a yard full of cattle which I needed to get out into paddocks and off hay as soon as possible, and I was aware of the tight timeframe for shooting the documentary. Preferably with a smile.

A few days after the filming was wrapped up, I got an email from Monica, one of the producers, checking in. Sally had mentioned that she was worried about me. I laughed. 'I was worried about me, Monica! It was a tough week, but it's done now. I'm okay.'

If I come across a little frazzled or ineloquent on film, don't be too hard on me. I'm probably quietly panicking on the inside about how I'm going to feed everyone for dinner ...

*

Leading up to Gossip Girl's twelve-month 'assessment' and our final filming segment in late June, we spent what time we could training on the weaners in the yards. Our cattle were slowly coming home in dribs and drabs, as the feed increased with follow-up rain. Though we had only received our 'average' rainfall for the season, average was enough. It was more important how it fell rather than how much, and most of our showers had been steady and soaking. As protective as I was of our newly grown grass, agistment of our cattle came at a cost and we had to find the balance. I dedicated an area of the property to holding our cattle while the rest of the country continued to be spelled. This end had received better rainfall than the rest and had responded well. I would pay it back with a long recovery period in due course. The time I spent at Cheela Plains had taught me a lot about managing our pasture and I was keen to start looking after it better. We couldn't implement the same cell-grazing practice, at least not in the short term, but the principles still applied.

We had a small mob of weaners come home that would be held in the yards on feed pellets until they could be bushed out into the bigger paddock with the rest of the weaners. In the meantime these were perfect trainers – fresh enough that Gossip had to be smart in how she worked them but pliable enough that she could have a win. Wishing we had another week or month under our belt to keep practising, the time drew near and Adam, Gossip and I headed to Perth for our flight to Darwin for the final shoot.

The final segment was filmed in the Douglas–Daly rivers region of the Northern Territory. It was quite the contingent of us that landed on the local caravan park. Neil and Helen McDonald, Peter Barr and the other participants, plus all the filming crew, on top of a bustling tourist business. The first day was pretty easy. We were instructed to stagger our arrivals at the Research Station where the filming would take place, so we waited till our designated times and then pulled up at the front gate. And waited. And waited. Joni, CJ, Frank, Rob and I, who were trying not to notice each other's dogs as instructed, were quietly sweltering away under the Territory's hot sun. Apparently, it hadn't got the memo about winter. Eventually, Rob's electric car with a broken alternator couldn't take the wait any longer and had to be driven into the admin block to go on charge while we waited for technical issues with the film crew to be resolved. Finally, we drove into the lawned area one at a time and greeted the 'judges' like we hadn't spent the night before catching up over drinks. I don't think any of us are going to win an award for our acting skills.

*

I can say in all honesty that before our trip to Darwin I did not know anyone with working dogs who had ever attended a dog's birthday party. Now I know quite a few. In celebration of the pups turning one year old (a week after we filmed but close enough) there was a birthday party thrown in their honour, complete with hats, a shaky rendition of 'Happy Birthday To You' and specially purchased doggy birthday cakes. Although the cakes looked the part, I'm sure a candle stuck in a juicy piece of steak would have been much more enthusiastically received by these farming pups.

Day two of the filming found us completing our final major assessment for the documentary. We were to demonstrate a 'stop and sit' command on our pups (the best I could hope for was a slight pause), that we could walk past a mob with our pup off a leash (more doable), and that we could shift a mob of 40 weaners through a gateway and back again (tentatively hopeful we could ace this one). Collars were drawn out of a hat to see who would go first and the day began. It was enjoyable to watch the pups at work. Trunk (Joe Spicer's young dog from the same litter as the other pups) and Lucifer did really well considering they were from the cold southern states and weren't used to the heat. Joni and Frank had great runs with Chet and Annie, demonstrating good stops and control over their dogs, and CJ had a good run with Spice. Gossip Girl and I, well, I reckon we passed. I was really proud of her efforts, even if we weren't the neatest or prettiest. She did well and tried her heart out ... with minimal heel bite.

*

Our final day of filming was at CJ's place a little further up the road. It was a lovely property with a stunning view over the surrounding area, and was definitely going to make for a picturesque finish. Between interviews, a fun test was sprung on us to see who could jump off a quad bike, open a gate up into a paddock with cattle sitting nearby, close the gate and return to the bike in the fastest time, all without their dog leaving the bike. What followed was a fun half hour as we tried to sabotage each other's runs, but the clear winner was Frank and Annie; Annie would not budge off the bike she had been instructed to stay on, despite our best efforts.

Although this wasn't a competition as such, Frank's Annie was fairly crowned the most advanced pup of the litter, and rightly so. She was a great little bitch, very talented and tuned in to what Frank would ask of her. It was Joni's dog, Chet, that I secretly wanted to take home with me and Gossip Girl, though. Chet had some really good work in him that was already holding him up well in Joni's team.

The grand finale of the filming was to be our five pups out gathering and working a mob of 100 weaners together in a paddock as the sun slowly set in the background. Sounds lovely, right? That's not quite how it happened. I feel it is worth pointing out that this is not something any of us would ever do in a normal situation. We would never take five twelve-month-old pups of differing skill levels out onto a mob with no experienced dogs to hold things together, let alone with five people out the front trying to work in sync. Ideally it would be one young pup with a few older dogs at a time, so the pup could make mistakes and the older dogs could help fix them. But we had one shot at this before the sun set so we had to make it work.

It wasn't the smooth grand finale that the producer had in mind, with all the pups working seamlessly together as the cattle gently flowed towards the gates, but that's life. The sunset was unbelievable, the pups thought they were on top of the world, the fences remained intact, and Gossip Girl worked like a little champion. At the end of the day, that was enough.

Later that evening, before everyone departed the next day back to their respective homes, we were shown a rough preview of the first episode of the documentary. It was brilliant. I won't lie; most of us being filmed in the documentary had niggling concerns about how we'd be portrayed over the course of the show. But the humour they included throughout the story added an authenticity to the show that made the mistakes and missteps okay. Meeting the guy behind the editing process, who sees every clip and hears every voice recording, was reassuring too, even as he told me I say 'hooly dooly' so much when things go wrong that he's adopted the habit himself now. I don't even know where that came from!

I hope everyone enjoys the show for what it is: a celebration of the wonderful working dogs that are essential to so many areas of agriculture in Australia. Though it's early days yet, Gossip has won me over with her cheeky personality and sparkling intelligence. Her work continues to improve, her understanding of the job at hand is helping her find the right place on the mob, and, as she matures, her penchant for cheap shots and dirty bites slowly abates. She has a spot in my team and I can't wait to see the dog she will become with another twelve months' experience behind her. I know how special these clever dogs like Gossip Girl are. I have been lucky enough to have had a few pass through my life and each has left their mark in their own way. As I know Gossip will.

Gossip Girl enjoying the running house creek.

Chapter Eighteen

The Other Side

'Keep asking questions so you are always looking for answers.'
– Anonymous

If I had known just what a mammoth task I had set for myself when I agreed to write a 60,000-word book, I'm not sure I would have ever started it. Turns out 'three hours a week' as originally proposed wasn't nearly enough time to get all my stories on paper for the original deadline. Luckily deadlines are flexible and publishers are patient.

Reflecting on my life and putting it into words on a page has been an incredible experience, especially as I look back over my journey with my dogs. We often get so caught up in where we are going we forget to appreciate where we have come from. To celebrate the little wins along the way, instead of holding out for the big milestones. I am grateful for every lesson I have learnt and every dog that has come into my life, even if only for a short time. For the opportunities I have had to travel, experience and grow alongside my team. We've made plenty of mistakes, me most of all. And I will no doubt make many more as the years pass. But when I think back to that first year, it reminds me a lot of writing this book. Sometimes it's better not knowing what you've got ahead of you or you may never take that first step. And I'm so glad I did.

I have to give full credit to my first dogs – Diddy, Ang, Julia, Flora and the handsome pup Zen – for their patience and tolerance with me while I learnt the ropes. They really did have the unenviable task of training me and holding the show together while I bluffed my way through from one situation to the next. But I wouldn't change any of it. I believe I am a few years ahead of where I would be if I hadn't gone all in. By starting with a team of dogs that already knew how to work livestock, they were able to teach me so much. It took trial and error and lots of patience on their part. But when we got it right and everything flowed, it was like hitting the jackpot. And it's those highs that get us through the lows.

Working with dogs, especially a team of them, isn't for everyone, and I fully respect that. For my own part, I wouldn't be on a property without them. Some people say using dogs makes you lazy. There are times when I'm standing at the gate watching the dogs do the work to bring the cattle into the yards and I can feel exactly that. But being able to utilise dogs to make a job easier is the reward for the time I spend every morning and night looking after them. Lazy? I'd call that smart. They pay my time back ten-fold.

Somewhere along the way, my dogs' influence on our livestock became more profound than I thought possible. During one of the lowest points of the drought, as we sent our cattle to wherever we could find a sale or some feed, there was a silver lining that helped keep me going. We received feedback from nearly every place they landed, praising their temperament and ease of handling. Even people who had previously sworn off Brahmans after a negative experience with them were converted. Folks I hadn't personally met would get in touch out of the blue to compliment us on the quality of our cattle and offer to take more. A close friend who was looking after some of our animals while they were agisted on farms nearby, would send me videos marvelling at their toughness and stoicism. From a fellow dog person, with her own well-educated stock, this feedback meant the world. What made the comments all the more poignant was knowing people were seeing our cattle at their worst and yet their best was still shining through.

I rang Neil McDonald one night while I was on the road heading north to thank him for setting me on this path. When I started with dogs and took on the challenge of educating our cattle, I had no idea how far-reaching that decision would be. I have no doubt that the temperament and adaptability of our cattle to settle into new environments, tolerate different styles of handling and cope with high levels of stress was what got us through the drought. It opened doors and offered opportunities that otherwise wouldn't have been available to us and these were lifesaving. Literally.

*

All through the drought, Murray and I talked about what we'd do when we got to the other side. It was the light at the end of a dark tunnel that we kept holding on to. The timing of the RCS course was fortunate in many ways, even if we couldn't start implementing a lot of what we had learnt. But it helped us pull into focus the direction we wanted to take both our properties in, as well as our business: regeneration of the country, financial security and to create a legacy that future generations want to be a part of.

Murray and Del now have three beautiful children. Murray's goal on the farm is to create a year-round green-growing productive system, incorporating well-known ecologist Allan Savory's holistic-management techniques. Murray's focus is on keeping living roots in the soil and vegetative cover above it for as long as possible, while avoiding a reliance on chemicals and artificial fertilisers. Planting perennials and adjusting his grazing strategies is just the start of his plans, which also, as he recently admitted, might just include a kelpie or two.

Mum is as passionate about the regeneration and rehydration of Glen Florrie as I am. She often talks about her grandfather, Robert Lukis, who was a man ahead of his time. While writing this book, I stumbled across an audio interview with Rob in the Battye Library, recounting his life story, recorded just one year before he died. His memory was unbelievably sharp, as he recalled names, places and dates in astonishing detail. Listening to my great-grandad's voice from beyond the grave, talking about his experiences owning and managing stations, the struggles and triumphs, was astonishing. I wish I'd had the opportunity to meet him but he has left the gift of his knowledge in his words.

On Mundabullangana Station near Port Hedland, which Great-grandad managed for twenty years from 1945, he took great pride in repairing the damaged landscape. Over his time, with help from field officers from the agricultural department, he reclaimed 174,000 acres of 'poverty bush country' through fire and deferred grazing and pulled a plough '2000 miles in two years' as he rehabilitated bare claypan flats. There would often be field days held on the station to share the results of this work with other managers, and he notes in his memoirs that he found it concerning that some didn't see the value in time spent on rehab work when a profit could be made, regardless. His response, I think, is profound: 'God alone knows what you are missing and I am gaining through the personal satisfaction of improving something that was crying out for improvement.'

*

Watching the biodiversity disappear around me just as I was finally starting to notice it was a hard pill to swallow. I had never consciously appreciated the complexity of our country, my focus always on the cattle rather than the landscape that supported them. I had no interest in learning about the different plant species beyond what we considered our two main sources of feed, buffel grass and birdwood grass, both of which are introduced. There is a saying in the regenerative world that you should love your country, not your cattle. Some take this further and say you should love your soil first. If you are focusing on your soil health, your land and your cattle will both be better off for it.

My interest in a more regenerative-focused management style was stoked after listening to an audio book called *Dirt to Soil* by Gabe Brown. I followed this up with Allan Savory's *Holistic Management* manual, which had me looking at the world around me in a new light. Often it seems to take something momentous to inspire change in the way we view the world. Now, as we stumble out the other side of drought, it feels like we have a world of possibilities in front of us.

Our long-term plan is to focus on rebuilding our biodiversity. We have already taken small steps towards this by creating what I call 'ethical bird baths' at our water points, in fenced-off areas cattle can't access, so even when we have the water troughs shut off to discourage cattle from lingering in an area, the bird, lizard and other animal life can remain. Leaving ground cover to help improve our water infiltration rates and provide protection to our soil from our extreme heat and heavy summer storms is one of our biggest goals. Repairing our water cycle and rehydrating the country, reversing much of the damage our roads and fence lines have caused through erosion, are other goals. On the areas where there is compaction, bare ground and open stony flats, many of which are old scars from the sheep-raising days, we will try a few different techniques to encourage revegetation. Fencing off small areas into exclusion zones will help us monitor the effects our management practices are having.

One way we can have a huge influence on the condition of the country is, unsurprisingly, how we manage our livestock. And that is where my kelpies will really come into their own. Mine and Adam's, as he slowly puts together a team of his own. Moving away from hiring in a large crew each year, we want to adjust our management style to really utilise the skills of the dogs. As we give the country more recovery time, shifting our stock more often so different areas get a chance to recover between grazing periods, rather than the traditional 'set stocking' that our station has experienced until this point, the dogs will be crucial. It won't be without its challenges, the unusual shape of our property being just one of these. But by utilising the dogs to help us reduce mustering and staffing costs, it's a feasible management option.

Over time, I would like to fence off our main river system into a wide laneway that extends across a large portion of our property, allowing us to move cattle easily as well as protecting our fragile river country from preferential and damaging grazing. This almost-backward step towards droving fits in with my desire to reduce our reliance on trucks and diesel. After learning more about electricity than I ever wanted to know at Cheela Plains, I intend to educate our cattle to respect hot wires so I can hold them in temporary night yards as we drove them long distances.

Eventually, inspired by stories and videos of KLR founder and teacher of Low Stress Stock-handling methods Jim Lindsay, I would like to be able to muster our cattle into temporary hot-wired yards and draft them up into lines with minimal reliance on steel panels, which are costly to buy, heavy to carry and time-consuming to shift. A lofty goal, to be sure, but with the correct handling and education of our cattle, as well as eliminating the infiltration of feral stock, it is not outside the realm of possibilities. Nothing is really; we are only limited by our imagination and our desire to give it our best shot.

We are still in the early days of incorporating maremmas into our program but I believe there is so much potential here. If, one day, I can have guardian dogs working across our property, living with and protecting our breeder cattle as well as our weaners, I will have realised a personal dream. Time will tell if this is a real possibility or remains just that, a dream.

*

As daunting as this can all seem, especially for a property spanning such a vast area, I take heart in knowing we won't be doing it alone. I heard New South Wales grazier David Marsh say something that really resonated with me on a Regenerative Journey podcast with Charlie Arnott: 'I used to see myself as the agent responsible for healing the land. Now I see myself as someone observing the landscape healing itself.' The relief in realising we don't need to have all the answers for how to fix the land is huge. We just need to get out of Mother Nature's way so she can heal herself.

It is not going to be all smooth sailing from here. I know there are a lot of learning curves up ahead, some sharper than others. But I am excited about the future. My family and Adam are as enthusiastic as I am about our new direction, and through the networks we have developed, I know there is a wealth of knowledge and help just a phone call away. But most of all, I'm excited about where the future will take my dogs and me.

I know we haven't seen the full potential that my working dogs can reach. But more than that, these hard-working and ever loyal dogs are the centre of my world. They have been my confidants and my allies, a steady, calming presence through the tough times, and contagious with their joy. When I'm feeling overwhelmed by life, my dogs help ground me and remind me I have so much to be grateful for. And I know I really do.

No one knows what the future holds, all we have is today. But no matter what direction life leads me, I know I will always have the incredible Australian kelpie by my side.

Teesh's Tips and Tricks

'Your training attitude should always be:
"It's you and me, dog, against the world".'
– Dana Mackenzie, dog trainer

'There is no such thing as a dog trainer. You are a situation creator.
You create a situation where a dog does something by reason of
"natural instinct". You then label the action the dog is about to take.
If you are consistent enough the dog will eventually correlate that
command with that action and no longer treat the learning –
note I said learning, not training – as an imposition.'
– Neil McDonald

Often it seems like we have this subconscious belief that we
are all born with instinctive knowledge of how to train a

working dog. We get a pup and think the rest will be easy, and sometimes it is, with the right pup, the right situation and the right attitude. But acquiring the knowledge to select the right pup, the skills to set up the right situations and the wisdom and patience to maintain the right attitude is where many of us come unstuck. And it's where working dog and stock schools really show their full value. They aren't just there to teach the dog what to do and how to do it, but to show us how to set up our dogs to learn and get the best chance of reaching their full potential. And I wouldn't be where I am today without the patience, guidance, knowledge and generosity in sharing that wisdom of great dog trainers like Neil McDonald.

I do not consider myself a dog trainer. If I'm honest, as much as I enjoy watching my dogs and pups progress, learn and really grow into what they are destined for, I find it hard to get enthusiastic about the nitty-gritty day-to-day education sessions. I much prefer taking my dogs with me to learn on the job. Hence, why I rely on my dogs having very strong natural instincts. I don't set out to 'teach' them what to do, my job is to set up the situation for their natural skill to come through, allow them opportunities to learn from their mistakes and protect them from any serious injury or knocks to their confidence while they are still finding their feet. Guess you can call these 'learning sessions at work'.

One thing I've learnt over the years, by attending a few different dog schools, is that it's as important to identify what you don't want to do as it is to identify what you do want to do. I've attended a school where the teacher's style didn't really suit me, but it still had value in teaching me what I didn't want to do. I was also able to pick up tips that have been valuable in my handling of different dogs that have come through my team over time. Every dog is different and what may work with one can be less effective with another. So having a few tricks up your sleeve that have the same end goal can be very handy.

Choosing your dog

I often get asked how I select a pup from my own litters. I have often asked this question of other breeders too – and everyone has a different system which works for them. For me, when selecting my next teammate I choose the pup who I sense I can have the best bond with. Usually, I already have an idea of whether I want a bitch or a dog pup, but this doesn't always go to plan, either due to having all-male litters when I want a girl or finding myself drawn to a different pup from the one I originally intended to keep. (On a side note, someone needs to research the link between how many females you are hoping for, and how many males you are likely to get, because I'm dead sure it's a real thing. Or maybe my dogs just love having the last laugh.)

I learnt quickly that when buying a new pup, it is important to do the research on which breeder has the type of dog and temperament that I am after. The type of work the dogs are doing and the style of handler the breeder is will tell me a fair bit about what I am buying. As you will know by now, my style of handling is minimal commands requiring independent thinkers, and my personality sees me getting along better with softer-natured 'sooky' dogs. Not easily offended soft, but I don't have the body size or deep voice that is dominating to a dog. So arrogant hard-headed dogs generally do my head in, whereas they might be perfectly suited to someone with a different personality.

If I am purchasing an older 'going' dog, finding one that has been trained and raised in a similar way to my own makes the adjustment so much easier. Dogs that have previously been communally fed generally fit straight into my camp system, after the obligatory initial round of introductions. Taking on a mature guardian dog like Ringer made me realise the importance of teaching all dogs basic manners – like leading, being tied up, handled and kennelled – preferably when they are young. You never know when the situation may change and they are asked to deal with experiences and people they have never met before. Especially in the case of guardian dogs, who, in their role as protectors against outside predators, face the very real possibility of injury. While I can easily catch and tie Rafe up when I need to (like when my kelpies are in season and he wants to play Casanova), Ringer is a different matter. One of these days, though, I'll outsmart him and we'll be taking a quick trip into the vet to permanently fix any risk of future Hush puppies.

Often people put off picking up a pup until they have the time to train it. In all honesty, I don't believe pups need much stock training before they're around eight months anyway, apart from an opportunistic look at stock to see if the instinct is there. What's more important to me is making sure I have time to spend with my new pup to develop a strong bond. Pups can still learn basic obedience in this time, how to tie up, sit calmly in a kennel, ride a bike, communal feed. As Greg Prince puts it, 'Up to eight months of age, it should be all about letting the dog learn to learn.'

Time spent with the pup now is what sets us both up for the wins later on. We often put pressure on ourselves and our pups to hit big milestones too early and we can come undone with our good intentions. A pup is like a young child. I want to set them up for wins, encourage every attempt and build their confidence to think they can do anything. Make them think they are ten feet tall and bullet-proof. Later on, this confidence will help them roll with the kicks and blows, mishaps and mistakes.

There are plenty of things we can do together that will fill those eight months. Caught between wanting the pup to 'Hurry up and grow so we can go to work,' and 'Stay young! You'll never be this cute again,' I like to let my pups be pups while they still can. Plenty of time for work ahead.

I had a couple of close calls with Gossip, working her too soon on our poddy calves. Though they were a quiet trainer mob, if a pup works in too close or tries to bite where it shouldn't (also known as taking a cheap shot), the cattle will still be inclined to have a kick at the offender. That hadn't been so bad when they were younger, but when our once small calves turned into large weaners they could pack a punch with one lucky strike. Normally, I wouldn't let a pup Gossip's age work them, but, as you know, at that time there was little choice.

Teaching commands

Once I have the measure of a young pup's working instinct on stock, a call off is the most important command I will teach it. Peter Barr has a great method for teaching a solid call off, and I have found it also helps to make sure that a call off doesn't always mean the end of the fun. These pups live for stock work and, if being called always means it's time to knock off, it's not long before they start getting a bit cagey about it. So I mix it up, calling them off for a pat, a swim or a short breather before letting them go back again.

Greg Prince believes the most important learning session is in the first three minutes, so sessions on stock can and should ideally be quite short. Moving from job to job with a quick pat, drink and breather in between is a great way to keep a young dog keen to listen and excited to see what you have in store for them next. The main thing is to keep it fun for both of you.

Teaching a pup to sit is a tricky one. Not the actual training itself but the how, when and why. It's one of the first lessons we usually want to teach our pups and it's the first thing other people expect them to know. I've lost count of the number of times people have said, 'Sit,' to my pups, and I've had to say, 'They don't know that.'

The reason I don't teach my pups to sit too early is that I don't want to curb their natural instinct for herding by interrupting it all the time. I have seen a few pups who have been half shut down from a nervous owner overusing the stop, sit, and stay commands before the pup is really switched on. I think it's like teaching a young horse to stop before teaching it how to walk under saddle. You end up not going anywhere. Get the movement first, then work on directions and corrections later. It may involve a little more legwork to start with on my end to catch an excited pup, but if the pup is hard to catch, it's generally a good thing! It means I've got a keen pup with strong instincts and that's exactly what I'm after.

Most of my dogs learn to sit for food later in their life, if at all. However, one thing I have recently started asking my pups to do is to wait patiently for the gate/door/kennel to open. I don't use any word commands; I just wait until they are sitting calmly before they get the reward of release. It's a handy way of teaching them to control their excitement and it can start at a very early age.

Keep the weight off

One of the best pieces of advice I was given early on by Scott Amon of Barru Kelpies was to not let my pups get fat. 'Grow 'em slow,' were his words and they are wise. When my heeler, Leah, raised her one and only surviving pup, Annie, after a few complications, I wasn't aware of any issue with over-feeding and I provided extra supplementation on top of Leah's ample milk supply. We used to laugh at the pudgy little pup, who was so fat, she would get stuck on her back trying to roll over, which was probably fine, except she never trimmed up and problems developed when she was older. By the time she was about twelve months old, she started showing lameness in her front shoulders and required surgery to remove some cartilage that was causing pain. The vet suggested she may have been a little overweight while growing and there was no disputing that had indeed been the case.

The theory I work with is after about three months of age, it's important to be careful not to let pups get too plump because it can interfere with their growth like it did with Annie. They should be covered but a little lean, shiny-coated and full of energy but not over-conditioned. If they are carrying too much weight, their bones can grow too quickly and cause issues later.

I monitor all my dogs' weight by feeling over their hips. I don't want to feel sharp hip bones but I also don't want to be feeling fat dimples (looking at you, Charm). Some pups may be naturally lean and need extra food, so I monitor them as they go through different stages of growth to make sure their nutritional requirements are met. As my dogs get older, they generally need less to stay in decent working condition.

It is well known how important it is to keep pups exercised, mentally and physically, so they can burn off extra energy, especially for the fast-paced kelpie. It is also worth keeping in mind that they are still forming all their joints and bone structure so excessive exercise can be dangerous. I try to avoid letting them jump off heights that put too much stress on their legs when they land (or on their noses if they forget to put out their legs – happens all too often). I also keep their exercise gentle, not running them too far or too fast and over-taxing their reserves.

Tying up

My pups have an opportunity to learn to tie up on the back or ride shotgun with me in the front of the buggy or bike when I am exercising my older dogs or during small jobs. I have short ropes secured permanently in the back of my buggy – short enough that a pup can't reach the edge to fall off and find themselves in strife. One thing I learnt recently is that a pup's neck is longer than you think and not all necks are the same. Even though I had Gossip on a chain short enough that

I thought it couldn't possibly be an issue, my long-necked pup still managed to pull hard enough to reach the edge of the buggy tray and tumble over. I try to make my chains short enough to be safe and long enough to be comfortable, but safety has to come first.

The same approach applies to tying up a dog to yards or a fence. It is important to test the length and make sure the dog can't get tangled up and over something. Trust me, they can be creative. My first week of owning dogs nearly ended in disaster when one of the team, Ang, managed to scale our cattle-yard fence. I had chained her securely down low but left the length too long and the temptation of seeing stockwork happening on the other side of the solid rubber fence was too much for her. Luckily for both of us, her long legs allowed her to reach the ground with the tips of her toes till I noticed her dangerous situation and remedied it. Though short chains or ropes can seem callous, the safety they offer is an important kindness.

A really good trick if you have to tie your dog to a parked vehicle, which I learnt from Neil, is to tie the chain around the base of a tyre. Often a vehicle is the only shade available and up here our dogs take any escape from the heat they can find, but it is also risky. If the vehicle needs to be moved in a hurry and someone doesn't realise there is a dog attached, it generally ends in heartbreak. With the chain secured on the ground but encircling the base of the tyre, the vehicle can drive over the chain links keeping the dogs on the chain free to get out of harm's way. A very handy and potentially life-saving strategy that every dog owner would do well to remember.

Keeping our dogs tied up or kennelled when they aren't supervised or working is part of our job of keeping them out of mischief and danger, especially young dogs. I will confess, I bend the rules a little on this, though. Most days I usually keep out an older dog that I trust not to wander to the yards so they can have 'house privileges'. I also have a different pup out each day so they can spend some time one on one with me, learn to be away from the others and have a change of scenery from the kennels. Each morning and night, though, all my dogs are taken for a walk down to the river, up the nearby hills or wherever we decide to wander, so they can burn off some energy and get some fresh air. And I know, every evening when I lock them away, they are safe for the night and not getting up to unwanted mischief.

Learning to lead

Teenage deafness is a thing, even in dogs. Every single pup I have owned has, at some stage, decided there are more interesting things to do than heed my call. Without exception. It's a boundary-testing thing they all seem to have to do and one they grow out of ... mostly. Usually it hits at around the four-to-six-month mark. I recently learnt the benefit of a pup dragging a long rope; thank you, Gossip. Pups are faster and often cleverer than I am, so stacking the odds in my favour any way I can is my way forward. If I haven't attached a long rope and they stay elusively out of reach, I will pretend that something more exciting is happening elsewhere, calling and running in the opposite direction so they come over to check it out. Fair warning, though, this only works until they cotton on, which doesn't usually take long.

This is also a good opportunity to teach the pup to lead nicely on a rope. There should be no tension in the lead so I am able to hold it with a relaxed hand. Short, sharp tugs down low are the key here, till I have the pup's attention, then I'll praise the pup before continuing on. It may take a few walks but there is nothing more frustrating than being led around by a dog pulling hard on the lead and nothing more rewarding than walking together without the lead at all. It's a case of 'getting your Bluetooth working!'

Communal feeding

I don't think I truly appreciated the benefits of good camp manners until I saw multiple teams of dogs happily intermingling over food and fun while I was travelling. Once good manners are established in the camp, the flow-on benefits are endless. I believe one of the most important steps to achieving this is communal feeding.

Communal feeding is a good way of establishing an even playing field within the team. What I've learnt is there should only be one boss around the dog camp and that needs to be me. There should be no pecking order amongst the rest of the dogs; they are all equal. I change up which kennels they sleep in so they can't get territorial. The order of who gets put away first is deliberately random so they can't pre-empt me. Getting these little things right in the camp benefits the workplace. If they can happily share a feed bowl, they won't growl at each other or bicker while working.

I was fortunate that I started with a team of dogs that already communally fed and worked together. It was easier to introduce new dogs to the established system rather than trying to convert a team across, but that's still not impossible. If I was in that situation, I would start by teaching the dogs I think will take to it most easily by feeding them dry food in one big bowl. Get the system established with these dogs, then slowly introduce another one to learn the new rules. If the new dog starts acting aggressively, it gets a warning. If it continues, it gets put away and misses out. It might take a few days but if I am consistent they soon work it out.

In saying that, I've had two bitches, Chrissie and Jinx, who never took to sharing. That carried through to growling on the bike or in the cages on the ute if they had to share. Some dogs just have a bit more attitude. If their work is good enough, I can learn to compromise.

If I have dogs that eat more than their fair share or don't need as much to maintain their condition (middle-age spread is real in dogs, too), I let them out onto the feed bowl after half of it is gone or pull them off it earlier. Younger dogs or lighter framed dogs that need a bit extra can have early access or extra feed put into their kennels afterwards. However people go about establishing it, communal feeding is a great way to ensure dogs can live and work together without constant bickering, which leads to a nicer environment for everyone. It can also be the difference between a dog reaching its full potential and falling through the cracks.

I recall seeing two dogs working at a farm down south, both handy males. The young dog had been purchased with the intention of stepping up into the old dog's role as that dog slowed down, but thus far the new dog wasn't really making the cut. As I watched them working the sheep yards together, the older dog would take every opportunity to intimidate or rough up the younger male, establishing that he was the leader and this was his territory. The younger male couldn't get to the right spot, was constantly looking over his shoulder in fear of the older male and was only half the dog he had the potential to be. There was no communal feeding done with these dogs; they were allowed to be territorial and the old dog retained his established superior role. This is okay, as long as the younger male is also able to live and work on his own in a safe environment without fear of retaliation. A dog won't reach its full potential in a situation like that and if we don't realise what's happening, it's the younger dog that can be perceived as lacking. We have to ensure we recognise these situations and find a way to give our young dogs the best chance at a decent start – and our old dogs a respectful retirement.

Retirement

While I was in Alaska, I chanced upon a book called *The Cruelest Miles: The Heroic Story of Dogs and Men in a Race Against an Epidemic* by Gay Salisbury and Laney Salisbury. It was an incredible book about the diphtheria outbreak in Alaska in 1925 and how the sled dogs and their handlers beat the odds as they raced vaccine serum across the country to the city of Nome, saving countless lives. The authors went further than just this one famous feat and shared stories about these amazing dogs and the men and women who relied on them. Though many parts of the book had me in tears and battling homesickness for my own team in the Pilbara, there were two stories in particular that stayed with me long after I turned the last page. Here is how I recall them.

One was of a mailman who was found too late, huddled over what could have been his life-saving fire, matches still in his lifeless hands. The evidence of his disbanded team showed in the remnants of the harnesses strewn on the ground nearby. But next to him, with his feet frozen to the ground, sat his lead dog, refusing to leave his master's side even in the face of death. If that doesn't show the capacity for the love and loyalty these amazing animals are capable of, I don't know what does.

The other story was of an older dog who had been the leader of the sled team for most of his life. That position is given to the smartest dogs because they need to be able to pick a safe path, sometimes sight unseen in blizzards. The dog was starting to slow with age so the decision was made to retire him to a less important role in the team and let a younger dog step up and learn the leading ropes. That old dog fought the change of position, doing everything he could to move from his new place in the line up to his spot in the lead. When he realised he'd lost his place, the proud animal dropped his tail and hung his head low. Later that night, he was heard howling out on the frozen lake before laying his head down for the last time. 'He died of a broken heart, a regret I will live with forever,' said the sledder.

Every now and again you have the privilege of meeting a dog that is almost human in their personality and intelligence. If we are lucky enough, those dogs will give us their everything. The least we can do is give them the consideration and dignity in retirement they deserve. Every dog is different and the kindest retirement might look different for each one. Flora was due for retirement when I lost her to snake bite, but I already recognised she would never be happy being left at home or unable to join in the stock work she loved so much, even as her body grew weary. Her retirement was to be with a loving family where she couldn't see or hear what she was missing out on, and spending her days on comfortable couches and evening strolls instead.

As I type, Jasper is lying asleep next to me, content just to be nearby. He is the next in line of my dogs to be retired, though hopefully not for a few years yet. I know Jasper's loyalty to me is stronger than his love of work, thank god, as I'm not sure I could part with him. He will be happy in retirement as long as he can be riding shotgun with me and overseeing proceedings from the comfort of the buggy or free to relax on a comfy couch back at the homestead. A fitting retirement for such an amazing worker and one I know he will enjoy.

*

Above all else, the best I advice I can offer to someone getting into dogs or wanting to change their current camp set-up is to find a system that works for you and your dogs. It's easy to get caught up on how everyone else does it and trying to implement that at home. I'm the first to admit my dogs are not the best behaved. They don't always stay focused on me. There are days when they jump up when they shouldn't and don't listen when they should. But we are happy. I went through a stage of thinking my dogs were out of control. I became extremely strict with them, trying to imitate others and trying to change us into how I thought we should be. But I'm not someone else, and neither my dogs nor I were enjoying life. As Greg Prince said, 'Be yourself. Dogs can tell when you aren't.' So find that happy medium that suits you personally. In the end, you'll all be better off for it, even if it costs you a few dirty paw prints on occasion.

Acknowledgements

I've always wondered about the lists of acknowledgements at the end of a book and now I understand why they're so long. Creating a book is such a massive undertaking and takes the time and effort of so many more people than just the author. I can't thank enough those behind me on this book for their ongoing help and support, but I'm going to try.

I often tell Gossip Girl she bought so much chaos into my life – and that's really no exaggeration. Thanks to Monica for the opportunity to showcase kelpies and working dogs through the documentary and, consequently, this book. It's sure made for an interesting year!

Huge thanks goes to Mary Rennie, my ever-patient publisher from HarperCollins, who has helped this book evolve, change direction, rebuild and finally come to fruition long after the original deadline. Her understanding and acceptance of my time constraints managing the station between writing chapters and replying to emails made this possible, and my appreciation for her support and encouragement can't be overstated. Thanks also goes to Madeleine James from HarperCollins for getting the book through the final stages and throwing in some grammar lessons along the way.

If it hadn't been for the enthusiastic encouragement of Margareta Osborn when I was first presented with the idea of writing this book, I highly doubt it would have happened.

I can't thank her enough for her support, knowledge, reality checks and honest feedback. You know you have a committed friend behind you when they sacrifice two days of their time to comb through your manuscript with you over the phone. At least we finally had that long-awaited catch-up!

To Kristy, Wendy, Blythe and Emma, you guys have been my tireless cheer squad. Thank you for reading my roughest drafts, keeping me grounded, offering motivation when I needed it and essentially writing this book alongside me. It wouldn't have happened without you.

To Neil McDonald, who is the reason I have my dogs and am still working on the land today. Your influence not just in my life but in the working dog and livestock industry across Australia is a testament to your knowledge and skills, and generosity in sharing it far and wide. You raise the bar and encourage others to follow you, and I can't thank both you and Helen enough for being in my life.

To Mum and Adam and, from afar, Dad and Murray, who have picked up my slack and essentially had to run the station without me this year as I locked myself in the office trying to get words onto paper. I promise I'll be back on the job now! Thank you for holding things together and carrying the extra load while I've been MIA. This time when I say it's finally done, I really mean it!

To all my followers who have supported me through the years on social media, where I share my journey with my dogs via photos and anecdotes, thank you for encouraging me to tell my story and sharing my adoration of these beautiful dogs.

Finally, to my dogs. You sure make this rollercoaster ride called life an interesting journey and I wouldn't want to do it without you. Here's to all the learning curves, mustering shenanigans and 'hooley dooleys' heading our way.